Stitch 'n' Fix

Stitch 'n' Fix

Essential mending know-how
for bachelors and babes

Joan Gordon

GUILD OF MASTER
CRAFTSMAN PUBLICATIONS

First published 2009 by
Guild of Master Craftsman Publications Ltd
Castle Place, 166 High Street,
Lewes, East Sussex BN7 1XU

ISBN: 978-1-86108-656-3

Associate Publisher: Jonathan Bailey
Production Manager: Jim Bulley
Managing Editor: Gerrie Purcell
Senior Project Editor: Virginia Brehaut
Editor: Naomi Waters
Managing Art Editor: Gilda Pacitti
Designer: Alison Walper

Step-by-step photography by Anthony Bailey
Illustrations by Sophie Joyce

Set in Avant Garde and American Typewriter

Colour origination by GMC Reprographics
Printed and bound in China by Hing Yip Printing Co. Ltd.

Contents

1 Button up baby

2 Quick as a flash

3 Zip it

4 Seams simple

5 Hemmed in

6 Luxury babe

7 Fix it

Introduction

In our fast-paced modern lives, few of us have the time or the inclination to make or repair our own clothes as our parents and grandparents once did. Gone are the days of 'make and mend' and darning those old socks so that they last for years and years. Many basic sewing and mending skills have simply been lost by modern generations.

I'm sure most of us have some item of clothing that has been languishing at the bottom of the laundry basket waiting to have that tear patched up or that missing button sewn back on. And who among us, at one time or another, has not had some little clothing emergency – a broken strap or a snagged trouser hem – just when you've got a hot date or an important meeting to go to?

Well, if you don't happen to have an old-fashioned grandmother to show you how (or do the repair for you) never fear, *Stitch 'n' Fix* will show you how. When the buttons on that favourite shirt pop off or that seam splits when you're rushing to get dressed, don't ditch it, fix it and get more mileage out of your ready-to-wear wardrobe.

Within the pages of this book you will find practical information on how to sew on buttons, stitch a hem, undo stitching, replace a zip, and so much more.

For the complete novice who has never threaded a needle in their life, the Basic know-how section will guide you simply and easily through a broad range of easy-to-master techniques. For the more experienced sewer, you'll find some neat tricks for cutting corners throughout the book.

Each repair is illustrated clearly with step-by-step photographs or illustrations. Most of the repairs are sewn or fixed by hand because sewing emergencies usually happen when you're at work or play – not when you're conveniently standing next to your sewing machine (if, indeed, you own one). In other cases, such as replacing zips, the book offers both hand and sewing-machine techniques to solve the problem.

Different sewing emergencies, such as replacing buttons and fastenings or adjusting a hem, are grouped together in separate chapters so that it is easy to find

the relevant technique that will solve your repair dilemma. There's even a chapter for that ultimate emergency when you have no sewing kit to hand at all – but you'll be amazed at what you can achieve with the office stapler or a few safety pins!

This book also offers much more than just emergency repairs. If you need to adjust your clothes in any way – taking them in or letting them out due to a change in weight, for example – a range of useful techniques is provided. Plus, there are all sorts of ingenious tricks and tips for reviving your wardrobe, from reducing a gaping neckline to preventing a sagging derrière in an open-weave skirt.

If you're new to the art of 'do-it-yourself' clothing repairs, then the *Stitch 'n' Fix* will quickly become your sewing- and garment-SOS recycling book.

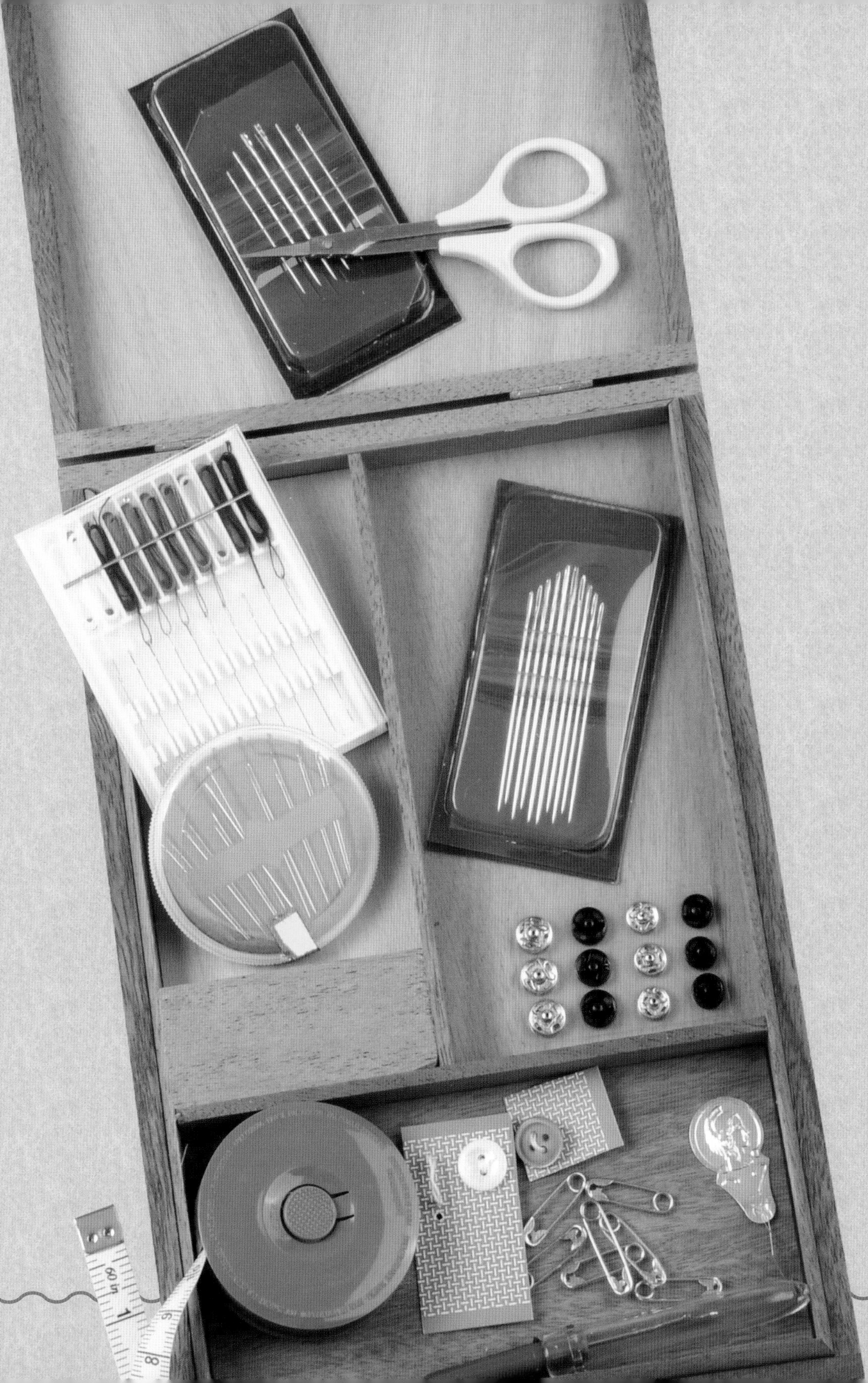

DIY repair kits

A stitch in time saves nine, not to mention several pennies. Stock up on a few basic pieces of equipment and sewing essentials and keep them handy in a storage box in the home for everyday sewing repairs. You may also want to make up a few mini sewing kits, to keep in the car or in your handbag, in your desk drawer at work, or to take on holiday.

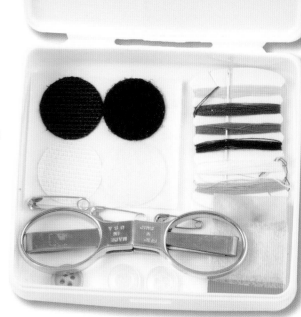

Sewing boxes

While department stores and haberdashery shops sell purpose-made sewing boxes and baskets these can be expensive, and there are a number of alternatives that you can find around the home. A plastic fishing-tackle box is ideal for holding lots of different small items in separate compartments. You could recycle a cardboard shoe box by covering it in wallpaper or fabric to match your own home furnishings. For a more elaborate sewing box – one that you would be happy to have out on show – visit a craft market or your favourite bric-a-brac store where you're sure to find something practical yet decorative.

Travel sewing kits

A miniature instant repair kit can be popped into a handbag or wallet. You can keep a more comprehensive one in your suitcase or in the glove compartment of your car. These compact kits will enable most basic emergency repairs when you're out and about.

Tightened security measures at airports and other international departure points mean that even the most innocent sharp object (such as nail clippers or small sewing scissors) may be confiscated from hand luggage. Thus it is best to put your travel sewing kit safely secured inside your check-in luggage.

Items for your travel repair kit

- Folding scissors
- Basic coloured threads wrapped onto card
- 2 x shirt buttons
- 2 x safety pins
- Iron-on hemming tape
- Self-adhesive Velcro
- A fine crewel needle

Your home sewing and repair kit

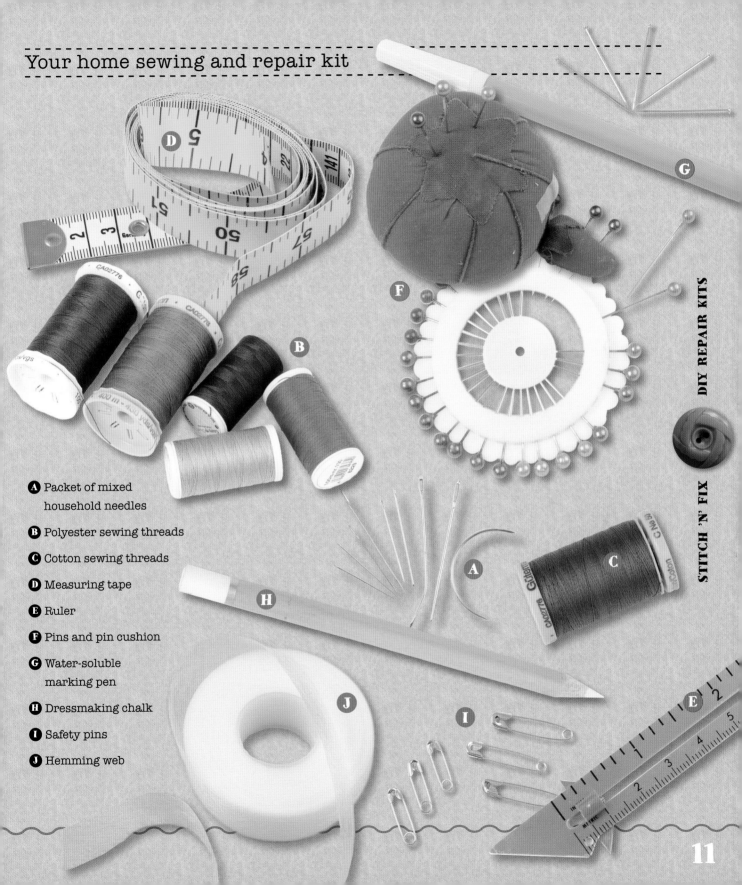

A Packet of mixed household needles

B Polyester sewing threads

C Cotton sewing threads

D Measuring tape

E Ruler

F Pins and pin cushion

G Water-soluble marking pen

H Dressmaking chalk

I Safety pins

J Hemming web

Needles

The finer the fabric you are working with, the sharper and finer the needle should be. Blunt needles will snag and damage the fibres in a garment.

Polyester and cotton threads

Use good-quality thread. Cheap threads are often made from short fibres and snap easily, causing seams to split. Reels of cheap thread usually have a slightly fluffy texture and lack sheen. Good-quality threads are spun from long strands of fibre. When you look at a spool of good-quality thread the fibres are smooth and give off a matt satin sheen. Always test a thread before sewing with it. Unwind a small section of thread from the spool, wind the free end around your middle finger and pull away from the spool. If the thread breaks immediately it is useless and should be discarded. Polyester thread is suitable for most sewing repairs; however, if you're making repairs to linen or pure cotton garments, it is advisable to use a cotton thread.

Dressmaking chalk

This is used for marking fabric. It is available in pencils that can be sharpened. The chalk marks can be dusted or sponged off the fabric.

Water-soluble pens

These pens can be used to mark stitching lines on fabric. When the marks are no longer required dampen a cloth or cotton bud and rub the fabric marks very gently until they dissolve.

Hemming web

This web is a very fine ribbon of glue that melts into the fibres of material when heated with an iron. Always read the manufacturer's instructions before use.

Hooks, eyes and snap fasteners

These items are all used as fasteners. They are made from metal or plastic, come in black, silver or transparent colours and can be bought in a variety of different sizes.

Dressmaking scissors

Sharp scissors designed to cut fabric. These scissors will become blunt if they are used to cut paper, cardboard or plastic.

Embroidery scissors

Small, sharp and pointed scissors – ideal for snipping threads close to the fabric without damaging the stitching.

Iron-on patches

Ready-made patches with heat-sensitive glue on the back. They can be used for an instant repair, frequently to denim garments.

Decorative patches

Embroidered patches that can be bought and hand-stitched to a garment.

Iron-on interfacing

This is a man-made fibre that is treated with heat-sensitive glue on one side. It is ironed onto the inside of a garment to give the fabric more body and stability.

Fabric glue

There are several fabric glues available on the market. Purchase one that can be used on a variety of different materials and ensure that it dries clear.

- **K** Dressmaking scissors
- **L** Embroidery scissors
- **M** Two- and four-hole buttons for shirts and blouses and shank for jackets
- **N** Hooks and eyes: small for blouses; large for jeans, skirts and trousers
- **O** Snap fasteners
- **P** Iron-on patches
- **Q** Decorative patches
- **R** Iron-on interfacing
- **S** Elastic
- **T** Fabric glue
- **U** Bias binding
- **V** Zippers: metal, invisible, nylon
- **W** Self-adhesive Velcro® dots and stitch-in tape
- **X** Thimble
- **Y** Needle threader
- **Z** Quick-unpick/seam ripper

Fabrics

Here are some of the most frequently used fabrics in ready-to-wear fashion garments. There are so many fabrics used in the manufacture of clothing that it would be impossible to feature them all in these two pages, but the ones covered here will help you identify those used in this book.

Linen is a durable and refined luxury fabric. It is the strongest of the vegetable fibres; it is double the strength of cotton. Not only is the linen fibre strong, it is smooth, making the finished fabric lint-free. When frequently laundered, linen becomes softer and finer in texture. Linen is made from flax; the fibre is extracted from the stalk of the plant. The lustre and sheen on linen fabric is from the natural wax content. The linen fibre can be easily dyed and the colour does not fade when washed. Linen wrinkles easily when worn but that is considered a part of its natural characteristics. Linen can be boiled without damaging the fibre **A**.

Cotton is a fabric that is in constant demand because it can absorb perspiration quickly, thus allowing the fabric to breath. Cotton fabric is often treated with permanent finishes to give a wash-and-wear property to garments. The cotton fibre is from the cotton plant's seed pod. The fibre is hollow in the centre and, under a microscope, looks like a twisted ribbon. Boiling and sterilizing temperatures can be used on cotton without disintegration. Cotton can be ironed at relatively high temperatures, stands up to abrasion and wears well. It is often found blended with other fibres such as polyester, linen and wool to 'blend' the best properties of each fibre **B**.

Silk garments are prized for their versatility, wear and comfort. Silk is the strongest natural fibre. Silk absorbs moisture, which makes it cool in the summer and warm in the winter. Silk is produced by the silk worm that once in the cocoon stage of its lifecycle is harvested. The cocoons are soaked until soft, a thread is extracted and then spun. Because of its high absorbency, it is easily dyed in many deep colours. Silk fabric retains its shape, drapes well and shimmers with a lustre all its own. Contemporary silk garments range from evening wear to sports wear. Silk garments can be worn for all seasons **C**.

Wool fibre comes from a variety of animal coats. The wool fibres have crimps or curls, which create pockets that give the wool a spongy feel and create insulation. The outside surface of the fibre consists of a series of serrated scales that overlap each other much like the scales of a fish. It will not only return to its original position after being stretched or creased, but will absorb up to 30% of its weight in moisture without feeling damp. Its unique properties allow shaping and tailoring. Wool is one of the most popular fabrics used for tailoring fine garments. Wool is also dirt and flame resistant. It is a resilient fibre that holds up to wear and tear **D**.

Polyester is a man-made fibre that is strong and resistant to creasing, which is why it is used in garment construction. Polyester melts at medium-to-high temperatures and must be ironed with care. It is manufactured in many weights. Threads spun from polyester fibres are strong, wear exceptionally well, and are used extensively in home sewing and manufactured sewing **E**.

A

B

C

D

E

STITCH 'N' FIX FABRICS

15

Basic know-how

Now that you have got all your essential tools and equipment together, there are a few basic techniques and stitches that you will need to master in order to make the repairs and alterations demonstrated in this book. If you have never picked up a sewing needle in your life, don't worry, these techniques and stitches are very simple and you will be guided through step by step!

Threading a needle by hand

the eye

the shaft

Step 1
Cut a length of thread approx. 18in (45.5cm) long and line the end of the thread up with the eye of the needle **A**.

Step 2
Slide the end of the thread through the eye of the needle and pull it through from the other side **B**.

Threading a needle with a needle threader

Step 1
A needle threader can be helpful if the eye of the needle is very small. Push the wire part of the threader through the eye **A**.

Step 2
Pass the end of the thread through the wire eye of the threader **B**.

Step 3
Pull the wire eye of the threader back through the eye of the needle **C**. Finally, remove the thread from the wire. If you run out of thread before completing your repair, knot off the thread and snip it close to the last stitch. Re-thread the needle and recommence sewing.

Making a knot 1 – using one strand of thread

Often, you will need to sew with a single strand of thread. Once your needle is threaded, leave one end of thread longer than the other and tie a knot in the long end. Alternatively, sew several stitches on top of each other to secure the thread before commencing to stitch.

Threading a needle by hand

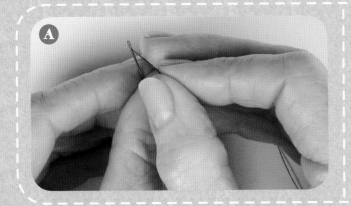

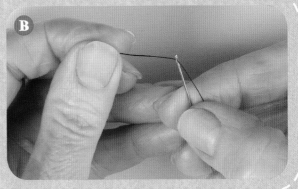

Threading a needle with a needle threader

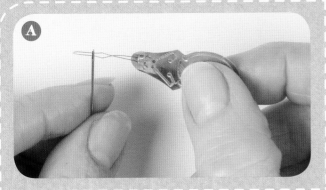

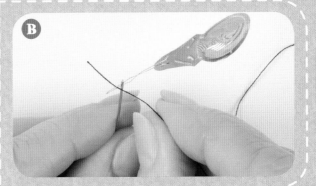

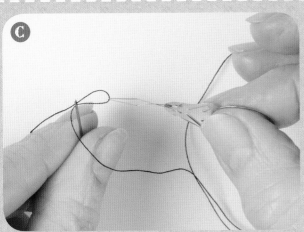

Making a knot 1

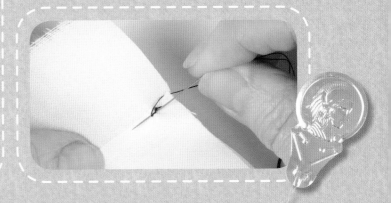

Making a knot 2 – using two strands of thread

Sometimes, perhaps when working with very thick fabric or when you are sewing through two or more pieces of fabric, you will need to work with two strands of thread for extra strength.

Step 1
Thread a needle, as shown on page 16 and pull one thread until both ends meet. Take the ends of the thread in your dominant hand and create a small loop.

Pull the length of thread to fasten the ends through and then into a knot **A**.

Step 2
Trim the tail of the knot **B**.

Undoing stitches

Quick technique

Step 1
Snip the stitch with the point of sharp scissors **A**.

Step 2
Flick the thread on the other side of the stitch up and away from the fabric with a pin or needle.

Using a seam ripper or stitch removal tool

Hold the stitch removal tool in your dominant hand. Slide the point of the blade under the stitch. Slide the stitch into the U-bend which is in the middle of the tool blade and push the tool forward and up slightly **B**. The thread will be cut by the fine blade in the U-bend.

STITCHES

There are six easy stitches that you will need to learn to complete your basic sewing repertoire: straight (or running) stitch; buttonhole stitch; slip stitch; herringbone stitch; back stitch; and zigzag stitch. There are also some stitches that are very easy to perform on a sewing machine.

Straight (or running) stitch

This stitch is used to sew two layers of fabric together.

Step 1
Using a soluble fabric marker draw the sewing line onto the fabric **A**. This line will help you to keep your stitching straight. If you're sewing two layers of material together then pin them first to avoid the fabric from slipping when stitching.

Step 2
Bring the threaded needle up to the top surface of the fabric.

Step 3
Make a small stitch **B** and then take the needle through to the other side of the fabric **C**.

Step 4
Leave a small space between the exit point of the first stitch and the starting point of the next stitch. As you bring the needle up to the top surface of the fabric ensure the point of it is in the middle of the marked line **D**. Make another little stitch **E** and continue sewing in this method until finished **F**. Create a knot at the end of the stitching and trim the thread.

Making a knot 2

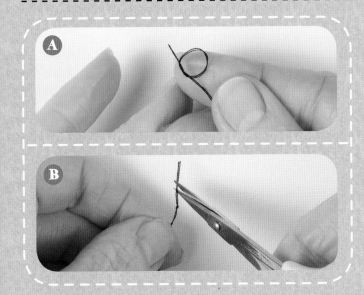

Undoing stitches

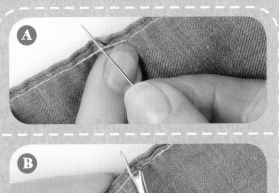

Straight (or running) stitch

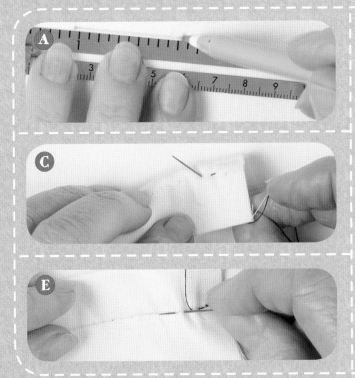

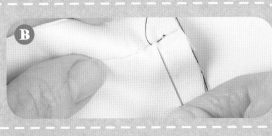

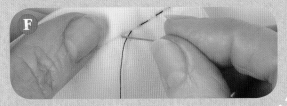

Buttonhole (or blanket) stitch

This stitch is used for making a buttonhole, sealing the raw edge of fabric and for attaching fastenings.

Step 1

Thread a sharp needle and knot one end of the thread. Working with the right side of the fabric facing up, diagonally insert the needle at the back of the buttonhole about ⅛in (2mm) from the cut edge of the hole. Bring the point of needle through the fabric into the buttonhole opening. Slide the thread under the point of the needle **Ⓐ**

Step 2

Pull the needle right through the fabric. The thread will have formed a small loop **Ⓑ**, sealing the raw edge of the fabric. Continue working stitches around the edge of the fabric or fastener. Place the stitches very close together to make a firm edge or space them for a more decorative look. When you have finished sewing, secure the thread to the wrong side of the garment with a knot.

Slip stitch

This stitch is widely used, as it is quick and easy to sew. Use it to take up hems, sew down a gaping facing and attach shoulder pads to the inside shoulder seams of a garment.

Mending a hem with slip stitch

Step 1

Work from right to left. Thread a needle with a long strand of thread that is the same colour as the fabric. Knot one end of the thread. Make a little stitch in the edge of the hem to secure the knot **Ⓐ**-**Ⓑ**.

Step 2

With the very tip of the needle pick up a few threads of the inside of the garment **Ⓒ**.

Step 3

Insert the needle under the hem fabric edge **Ⓓ** and pull the needle through the fabric until all the thread has been pulled through the strands of fabric.

Step 4

Slide the needle into the edge of the hem making a small stitch. Slide it along and bring it up and out of the hem close to the edge of the hem fabric **Ⓔ**.

Step 5

Repeat the stitch, picking up the threads of the garment fabric in the same direction on each stitch. Try to sew the stitches as evenly as possible, maintaining regular spaces between each stitch **Ⓕ**. When you have finished the stitching, create a small knot on the very edge of the hem and snip off any excess thread.

Buttonhole (or blanket) stitch

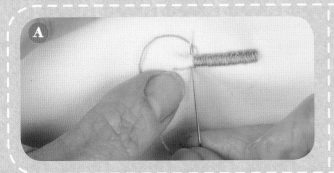
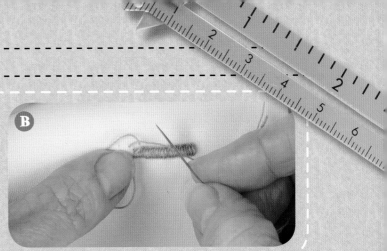

Slip stitch

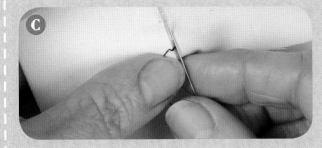

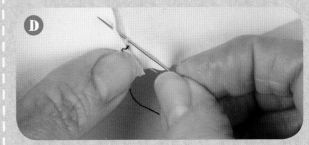

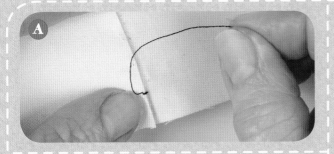

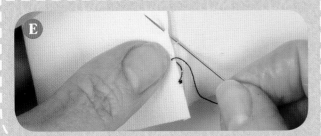

Herringbone stitch

This stitch is used to fix a single hem.

Step 1

Work this stitch from left to right. Start sewing by securing the thread with a few small stitches to the edge of the hem.

Step 2

Make a long, diagonal stitch from left to right across the raw edge of the hem and back through the inside fabric of the garment, about ¼in (6mm) from the hem edge **A**.

Step 3

With the needle pointing to the left, make a small stitch in the fabric of the hem, sewing from right to left **B**.

Step 4

Moving from left to right, now bring the needle up and out of the fabric and make another long, diagonal stitch. As you make this stitch the threads should cross over each other **C**. Continue to stitch until the hem is finished **D**. Keep the stitches evenly spaced and approximately the same size **E**.

Back stitch

Back stitch is the sturdiest and most secure of the hand stitches that are used to secure a seam or to sew two layers of fabric together. The method used for creating this stitch is similar to that used by a sewing machine.

Step 1

Work this stitch from right to left. Sew a few small stitches to secure the thread before starting to stitch.

Step 2

Make a small straight stitch and then leave a little extra space in front of the stitch you have just made before bringing the needle back up through the fabric **A**.

Step 3

Bring the needle up to the surface and stitch back towards the first stitch, filling in the space made in step 2. Take the point of the needle down into the exit hole of the previous stitch **B**.

Step 4

Repeat steps 2 to 3 until you have finished sewing the fabrics together **C**. Knot off the thread and snip the excess with scissors.

Herringbone stitch

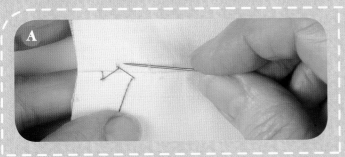

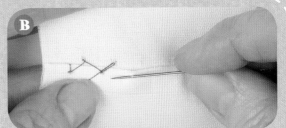

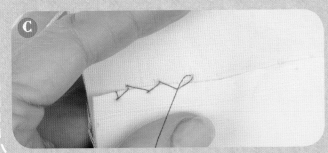

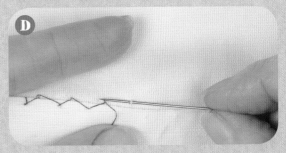

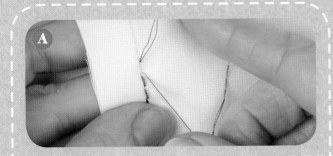

Back stitch

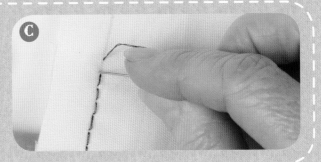

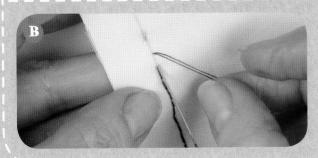

Zigzag (or overlock) stitch

This stitch is used to overcast the raw edges of seams to prevent the fabric from fraying when washed. It's also a useful stitch for joining the seams of stretch fabrics. The angle and distance between the zigzag stitches mean that seams, necklines and armholes, for example, can give and stretch without the sewing thread snapping.

Step 1

Thread a needle with polyester thread and knot together both ends. Pass the needle through the fabric close to the edge of the seam **A**.

Step 2

Make a diagonal stitch over the raw edge of the fabric. Bring the needle back up and out again through the base of the first stitch. Now pass the needle through the top of this stitch **B**.

Step 3

Sew neat little zigzag stitches, keeping them evenly spaced and fairly close together **C**.

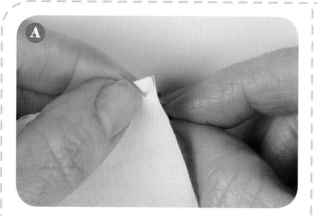

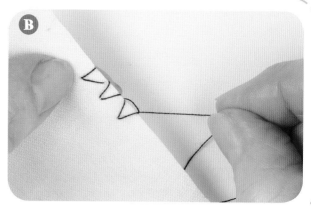

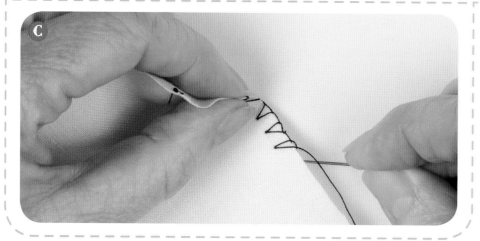

Sewing machine basics

The instructions in this book assume a basic level of ability with a sewing machine so always refer to the manufacturer's manual for instructions on maintenance and particular settings. You may find the illustration below handy to identify the main features of most basic machines.

Sewing machines, like all valuable tools, need to be kept clean and regularly maintained. If you have an old machine that hasn't been used for some time, it is advisable to take it to a sewing machine technician to have it serviced. The grease that is packed into the gear case can solidify over time and if this is not checked you run the risk of the gears seizing, which inevitably ruins the functioning of the machine. It's also a good idea to check in the sewing machine manual how to oil your machine to keep it in good operational order. Various man-made fibres such as polyester

will blunt the needle, so to prevent throwing out the timing of the machine, always change the needle on the machine every six hours of sewing. A good variety of sewing needles is vital. Purchase a case of mixed needles ranging in size from size 70, which is used for fine fabrics, up to size 90, which is more appropriate for sewing heavier weight fabrics such as denim.

If you are looking to buy a new sewing machine then it pays to shop around. Do your homework before you buy so that you purchase a machine that will meet your sewing needs. If the machine is only to be used for repairing clothing then a second-hand model will certainly fit the bill as long as it is in good working order. Basic functions to look for include a free arm that may be removed so that you have easy access to the leg of a trouser or shirt sleeve and an automatic buttonhole feature. Both functions are time-saving essentials.

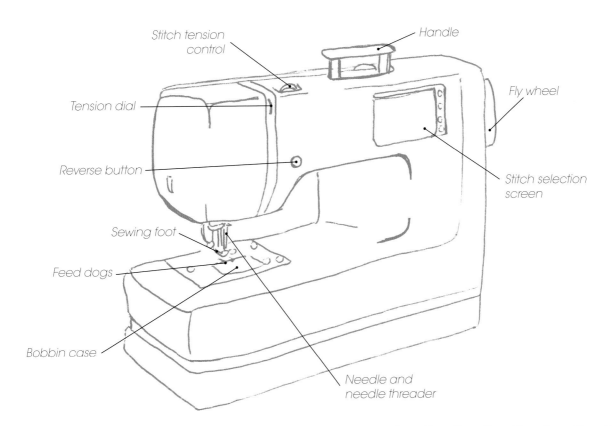

Stitch tension control

Handle

Fly wheel

Tension dial

Reverse button

Stitch selection screen

Sewing foot

Feed dogs

Bobbin case

Needle and needle threader

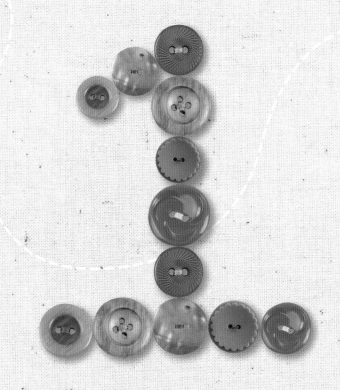

Button up baby

Sewing on a two-hole button

Probably the most frequently experienced clothing emergency is when a button pops off a shirt. In irritation we often end up putting the garment back into the wardrobe with the intention to sew the button back on, only to never get round to it. Fix it now! You can learn how to do it here, in five easy steps.

Step 1

Thread a needle with polyester thread similar in colour to the fabric of the garment. (The photos show contrasting thread being used, for clarity.) Knot the two strands of thread together (see pages 16–17 for needle-threading and knotting techniques).

Step 2

With one hand, hold the button in place where you intend it to be attached **A**. Working from the inside of the garment, push the point of the needle through the fabric where the original button was sewn on and then up through one of the holes in the button **B**.

Step 3

Pull the needle and thread up and out of the first hole in the button. Now place the point of the needle down into the second hole on the button **C** and push it through to the wrong side of the fabric. Pull the needle and thread gently until a small stitch of thread lies flat on top of the button. The needle and remaining thread are now on the inside of the garment **D**.

Savvy Sally says...

Buttons sewn onto shirts are usually attached by commercial sewing machines. These machines don't knot off the thread, which is why the buttons often fall off after several washes. When you buy a good-quality shirt, take the time to overstitch the buttons. Secure the buttons firmly to the fabric so that they last as long as the shirt.

Step 4

Repeat steps 2 **E** and 3 **F** several times, holding the button firmly in place as you stitch up, over and through the holes in the button.

Step 5

When the button is stitched securely into place, make a stitch just through the fabric on the inside of the garment **G**. Make a second stitch just through the inner fabric, inserting the needle through the loop **H** before pulling tight **I** to make a knot. Snip off the excess thread with scissors, close to the finished knot **J**.

DIY Repair Kit

- A fine sewing needle
- Thread to match the fabric
- A replacement two-hole button (if the original is lost)
- Scissors

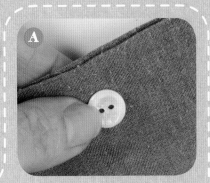

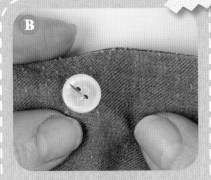

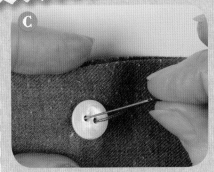

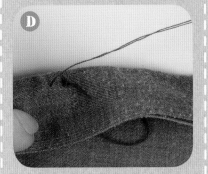

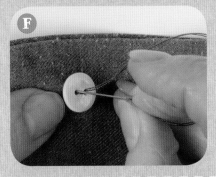

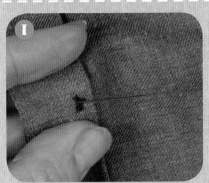

Sewing on a four-hole button

Buttons with four holes are most frequently used on men's business shirts. The four holes in the button require additional thread, which makes it a more secure fastener than a button with two holes. Sewing on a button with four holes employs much the same principles as those for sewing on a two-hole button (see pages 28–29). Once finished, you will have a neat cross of stitches across the centre of the button.

Step 1

Thread a needle with polyester thread similar in colour to the fabric of the garment. (*The step-by-step photos show contrasting thread being used, for clarity.*) Knot the two strands of thread together (see pages 16–17 for needle-threading and knotting techniques). Refer to the numbering of the holes in the button diagram when working through the following steps.

DIY Repair Kit

• A fine sewing needle
• Thread to match the fabric
• A replacement four-hole button (if the original is lost)
• Scissors

Step 2

With one hand, hold the button in place where you want to attach it. Working from the inside of the garment, push the point of the needle through the fabric where the original button had been sewn on and up through hole 1 in the button **A**.

Step 3

Pull the needle right up and out of the hole in the button and gently pull the thread until the knot is sitting flush with the inside of the fabric. Now take the point of the needle and push it into hole 2 in the button **B**. Work a diagonal stitch across the face of the button.

Step 4

On the inside of the garment pull the needle and thread until the first stitch made on top of the button lies flush and firm. Now make a small stitch to the left and take the needle up through the fabric and into hole 3 in the button **C**.

Step 5

Pull the needle and thread gently until all the excess thread is pulled through hole 3 in the button. Make a diagonal stitch across the face of the button, crossing the original stitch. Now push the needle down and through hole 4 in the button and pull the thread through to the inside of the garment **D**. You should now have made the first 'cross' of stitches across the top of the button **E**.

Step 6

Repeat steps 2–5 several times until the button is firmly attached to the garment **F**. Then make a stitch just through the fabric on the inside of the garment (see **G**, page 29). Make a second stitch just through the inner fabric, inserting the needle through the loop (see **H** page 29) before pulling tight (see **I** page 29) to make a knot. Snip off the excess thread with scissors, close to the finished knot (see **J** page 29).

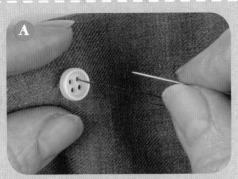

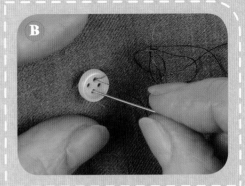

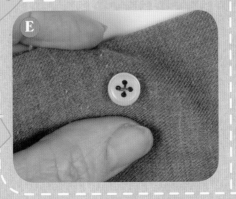

Practical Pete says...

Once you have finished sewing on the button, for extra security you can dip a pin into fabric glue and carefully rub the glue over the knotted threads to prevent them from unravelling. But be careful not to get the glue onto the fabric, as it will leave a permanent stain.

31

Stitching on a shank button

Shank buttons are used on jackets and coats. They often have a decorative face with a metal or plastic shank on the back. The button sits slightly up and off the fabric due to the size and depth of the shank. The shank is used to attach the button to the garment.

Step 1

Using dressmaking chalk, mark the placement for the button **A**. Thread a needle with some polyester thread matching the colour of the garment. (*The step-by-step photos show contrasting thread being used, for clarity.*) Knot the two strands of thread together (see pages 16–17 for needle-threading and knotting techniques).

Step 2

Take the point of the needle through a few strands of the material right on the chalk mark. Pull the thread so that the knot sits flush against the chalk mark **B**.

Step 3

Make a small fold in the fabric and hold the button so that the shank is just above the chalk mark and where you have pulled the thread through **C**.

Step 4

Hold the button. Pass the needle through the shank, down through the fabric of the jacket, making a tiny little stitch **D**. Bring the needle back up through the fabric and through the shank once more. Repeat this sewing action four or five times **E**. Don't pull the thread too tightly and keep the tension of the thread even. This will ensure that the button has a little bit of movement.

Step 5

Run the needle along through all the stitches you have made between the shank and the fabric **F**. Wrap the thread around the base of the stitches three times **G**. Push the needle right through to the inside of the garment **H** and tie the thread off to the inside of the garment securing it with a neat knot. Snip off any excess thread, close to the original stitching. You will now have a firmly attached and aligned button **I**.

DIY Repair Kit

- A fine sewing needle
- Thread to match the fabric
- A replacement shank button (if original is lost)
- Scissors

Making a buttonhole

To make a buttonhole is relatively easy. Before marking and cutting, make sure you measure the width and height of the button you wish to use. The buttonhole needs to be approximately ⅛in (2mm) longer than the width of the button for it to slide through easily.

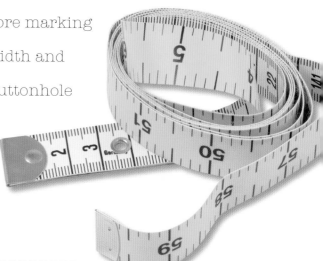

By hand

Step 1
Thread a sharp needle and knot one end of the thread. Working with the right side of the fabric facing up, diagonally insert the needle at the back of the buttonhole, about ⅛in (2mm) from the cut edge of the hole **A**.

Step 2
Bring the point of needle through the fabric into the buttonhole opening. Work from left to right. Slide the thread under the point of the needle. Pull the needle right through the fabric. The thread will have formed a small loop, sealing up the raw edge of the buttonhole **B**.

Step 3
Continue working stitches around the buttonhole edge **C**. Place the stitches very close together to make a firm edge **D**. When finished secure the thread to the wrong side of the garment.

With a sewing machine

If you know how to operate a sewing machine it's very easy to create a professional-looking buttonhole. Most modern sewing machines have a built-in, automatic buttonhole feature and a specific buttonhole foot

that either clips or screws on. Refer to your sewing machine's manual to find out if your machine has these features and how to use them. Make sure you use thread that matches the colour of the garment.

DIY Repair Kit
- Thread to match fabric
- Needle
- Scissors
- Fabric marker
- Tape measure

By hand

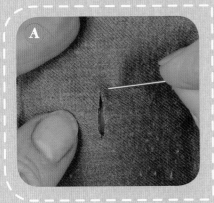

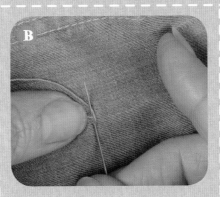

Savvy Sally says...

Woven, knit and stretch fabrics may require a small amount of interfacing to be placed between the facing and the outer fabric. The interfacing prevents the buttonhole from stretching. Always make a sample buttonhole on the same fabric before sewing onto the garment.

With a sewing machine

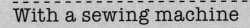

Repairing a buttonhole

On a good-quality tailored suit, buttonholes are traditionally stitched by hand. The buttonholes on most mass-manufactured garments, even expensive ones, are stitched by machine. Often the threads used are poor quality, hence the buttonholes fray, rendering the garment unwearable. Occasionally buttonhole stitching unravels because the stitches have been made too close to the middle of the hole.

Instant fix

If the garment is made from a textured wool or linen with an overall pattern **A** it can be temporarily fixed with a tiny amount of fabric glue or over-sewn with buttonhole stitch (see page 34).

Step 1
Carefully dip the tip of a pin into the fabric glue **B**.

Step 2
Now carefully run the tip of the pin over the stitches, being careful not to get any glue on the fabric of the garment **C**. Allow the glue to dry and the stitches will now hold until you have time to mend it with a needle and thread **D**.

Practical Pete says...

When repairing a buttonhole on a wool or tweed jacket use waxed quilting thread in a colour to match your fabric. Waxed thread slides easily through thicker materials and is less prone to twisting and knotting. It is available in good haberdashery stores.

DIY Repair Kit
- Pin
- Fabric glue
- Needle
- Matching thread
- Scissors

Create a new look with buttons

Jackets, coats, cardigans, skirts, trousers and dresses can take on a completely new look with the addition of decorative buttons. When doing an annual or seasonal wardrobe clear-out, remove the buttons for safekeeping before relegating any clothes to the recycling bin – buttons are expensive! Not only can these buttons be used on other garments, they can also be used to make jewellery or to decorate cushions and other home furnishings.

Make a dramatic statement with rhinestones or crystal

Create a classic look with pearls

A military or nautical style can be achieved with metal buttons

Designer buttons make a fashion statement

Novelty buttons are great for kids' clothes and accessories

For feminine appeal use floral buttons

Wooden buttons work well with natural fibres

Link shank buttons with fine chain to make unique cufflinks

Instant fix

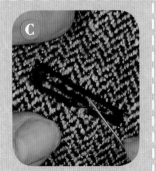

Sewing on hooks and eyes

Hooks and eyes are fasteners used to hold the edges of a garment together or to hold fabric together when it is overlapped. They are available in different sizes and colours to match different fabrics. Most hooks and eyes are made from metal for durability but synthetic ones are available. There are hooks and eyes that are suitable for blouses and dresses and sturdier varieties that are used to secure trouser and skirt waistbands (see page 40).

Most hooks and eyes are sewn in place by hand or with the use of a sewing machine. The no-sew versions must be clamped in place and involve the use of specific tools. These fastenings take more skill to attach to a garment and you should follow the instructions that are included with the package.

For edges that just meet, use either straight stitch or buttonhole stitch (see pages 18–20) to attach the hook and eye.

Attaching the hook

Step 1
Thread a needle with thread matching the colour of the garment. (The step-by-step photos show contrasting thread being used, for clarity.) Knot the two strands of thread together (see pages 16–17 for needle-threading and knotting techniques). Select a hook (and eye) that is suitable for the fabric. Place the hook on the wrong side of the garment about 1/10in (3mm) in from the edge of the finished seam.

Step 2
Start sewing the hook onto the material with a few stitches. Bring the needle up to the top surface of fabric **A**, across the bend of the hook and back down to the underside of the fabric. Try to stitch between the two layers of fabric so that the stitches don't show on the outside of the garment.

Step 3
Sew the loops of the hook in place with either straight or buttonhole stitches **B**. Stitch through the holes all the way around both loops **C**, then, coming up from the underside, stitch across the end of the hook again to hold it flat **D**.

Attaching the eye

Step 1
Align the sides of the fabric that you wish to fasten together.

Step 2
Mark the position for the eye with a water-soluble fabric marker, allowing the eye to extend slightly past the finished seam of the garment **A**.

Step 3
Using either straight or buttonhole stitch (see pages 18–20), attach the loop to the inside edge of the opposite side of the garment **B**. Continue stitching through both loops of the eye **C**, remembering to stitch between the two layers of fabric so that the stitches don't show on the outside of the garment. When the stitching is complete, finish off with a neat knot and snip off the thread with embroidery scissors.

Attaching the hook

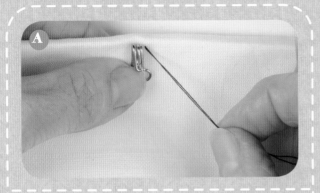

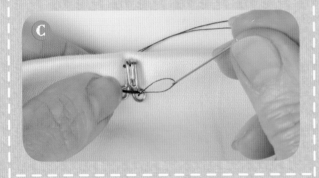

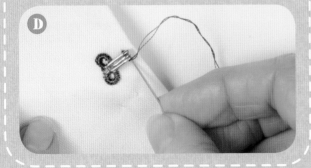

Attaching the eye

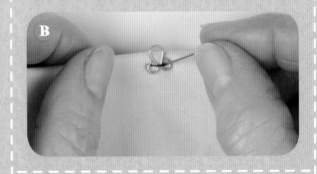

Sewing metal hooks and eyes onto waistbands

Metal fasteners are very sturdy and are usually used on the waistbands of trousers, skirts and other garments made from medium to heavyweight fabrics. They sit nice and flat on the inside of the waistband.

Sewing the hook onto a waistband

Step 1
Mark the placement for the hook onto the fabric using a fabric marker pen. Thread a needle with matching thread, then make a knot.

Step 2
Take the point of the needle down one of the holes in the metal hook. Bring it back up through the fabric a small distance away from the edge of the hook. Repeat this stitch several times, sewing in the same entry and exit holes **A**.

Step 3
When the stitching feels firm, slide the tip of the needle under the hook, through one layer of fabric and up into the adjacent hole and make several stitches in the same way **B**. Continue stitching until the hook has been attached securely through all its holes.

Step 4
Re-thread the needle and tie the ends of the thread into a knot. Slide the point of the needle up and through the hole at the top of the hook catching a few strands of fabric as you work. Bring the needle and thread right through the hole then sew back down into the fabric where you commenced. Repeat this stitch a few times and pull the thread so that the stitch sits firmly and neatly. Knot off the thread when finished sewing and trim off the excess thread with scissors.

Sewing the eye onto the waistband

Step 1
Overlap the waistband and position the hook onto the fabric where you wish it to connect with the eye. Mark the placement of the eye using a fabric marker. Thread a needle and tie the two ends of thread into a knot. Make a few small back stitches on one of the marks on the fabric.

Step 2
Make a small stitch in the fabric, bringing the needle up and through the metal eye **A**. Make several little stitches to secure it to the fabric **B**.

Step 3
Once the first end of the eye feels secure, pass the needle underneath the eye so that you can bring it out to the upper side of the fabric again to attach the other end of the eye **C**. Repeat step 2 until the eye is firmly stitched in at the other end **D**. Knot off the thread at the back when finished sewing and trim off the excess thread with scissors.

Sewing the hook onto a waistband

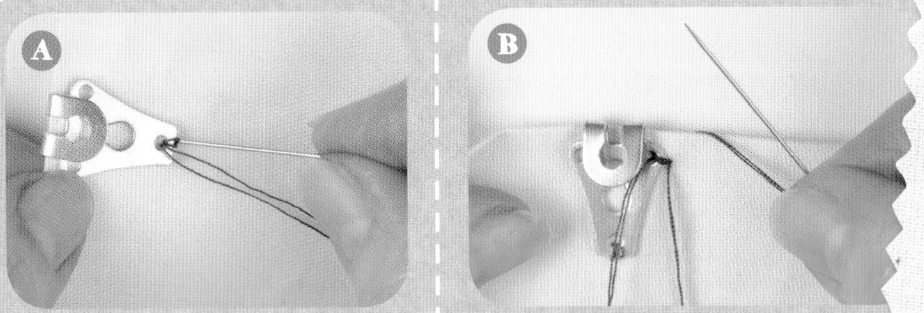

A

B

BUTTON UP BABY

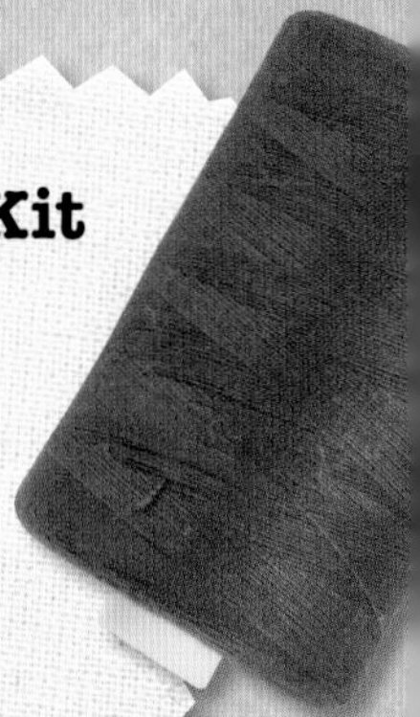

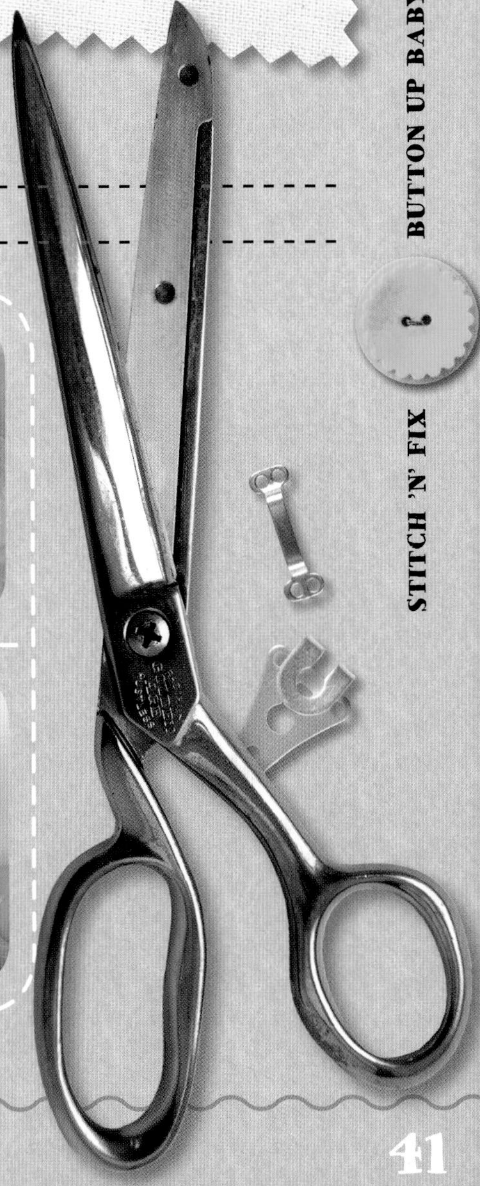

Sewing the eye onto the waistband

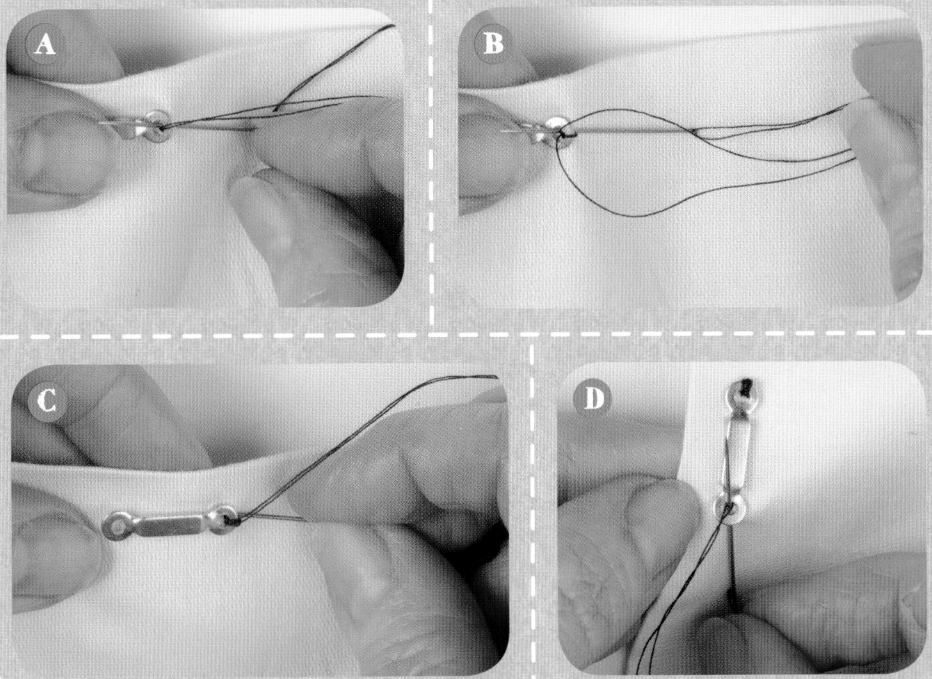

A

B

C

D

STITCH 'N' FIX

Sewing on snap fasteners

Snap fasteners come in several sizes for lightweight to heavyweight fabrics and are available in metal and plastic. They are used to close seams and to secure a closure where there is little strain on the garment, as they are not as strong as hooks and eyes. Snap fasteners come in two parts, the ball snap and socket, each placed on opposite sides of the closure.

Step 1

Mark the placement for the snaps onto your garment using a water-soluble pen **A**. The ball of the snap is usually placed about ⅒in (3mm) from the edge of the fabric if it is being used to close a seam.

Step 2

Thread a needle with thread that matches the colour of the garment. (*The step-by-step photos show contrasting thread being used, for clarity.*) Knot the two strands of thread together (see pages 16–17 for needle-threading and knotting techniques). Take the point of the needle through a few strands of fabric where you wish to attach the snap. Sew a few stitches on top of each other to fasten the thread.

Step 3

Pass the point of the needle through one hole on the snap. Pull the thread all the way through and take the needle back down an adjacent hole **B**.

DIY Repair Kit

- Snap fasteners
- Needle
- Thread
- Scissors
- Water-soluble fabric marker

Step 4

Bring the needle back up in the next hole and continue stitching around the snap until it is securely in place **C**. Try not to sew right through the top surface fabric as the stitches will show. When finished knot off the remaining thread and trim it with scissors. The socket is attached in exactly the same way on the other side of the closure.

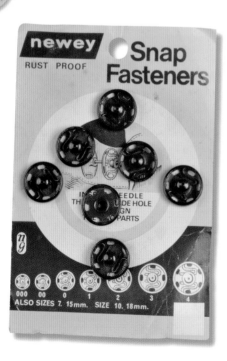

newey
RUST PROOF
Snap Fasteners

ALSO SIZES 7. 15mm. SIZE 10. 18mm.

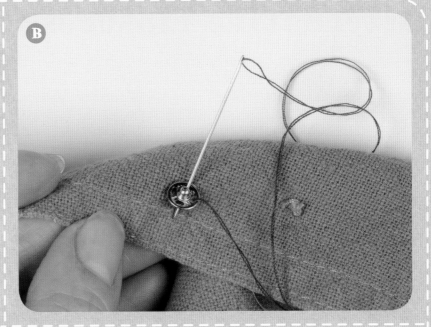

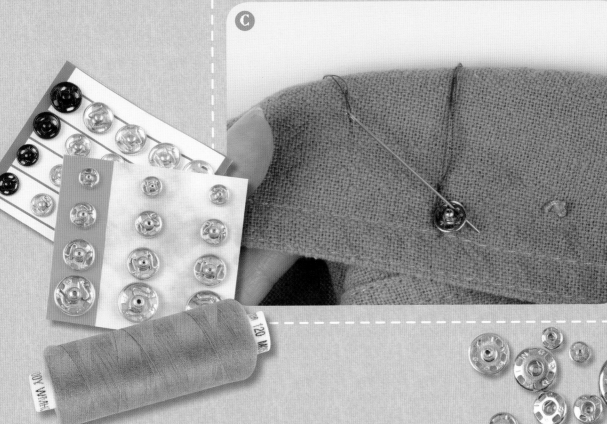

43

Alternative closures

It's easy to transform the style of a garment – plain buttons can be replaced with more ornate buttons, metal clips, corded toggles, ties, ribbons or with beads linked together with chain. Go window-shopping and look at how designers trim and finish their clothes. Unusual closures add a unique finish and touch of individuality to your clothes. A simple cardigan or jacket can take on a couture look just by a simple change of buttons.

Secure a cuff on a shirt or fasten a waistcoat with buttons or beads linked with chain. Necklaces or old bracelets can be pulled apart and reconstructed to make fancy linked closures **A** and **B**.

Metal clips used for attaching braces to trousers can be used creatively to replace the buttons on a jacket or side closure of a skirt. When window-shopping, observe how designers add a unique touch to a garment with fancy closures **C** and **D**.

Metal clasps add a professional and expensive-looking touch to denim skirts and waistcoats **E** and **F**.

A silk toggle can give an ordinary jacket an elegant oriental look **G** and **H**.

Large wooden buttons secured with soft cord add designer interest to an otherwise plain garment **I**.

See page 37 for more examples of the variety of buttons you can find to transform your clothes.

Practical Pete says…

Collect unusual buttons, clips and toggles and store them in a small box. Vintage shops are often a gold mine for finding unusual closures.

STITCH 'N' FIX

Sewing on Velcro closures

Velcro is a nylon product that consists of two surfaces which grip when pressed together. One surface has a rough surface made of little hooks while the facing surface has soft loops with a slightly raised pile. When the two layers are pressed together the hooks interlock with the loops. Velcro comes in the form of strips or dots and can be used to close pockets, waistbands and front fly closures, as well as to attach a range of other everyday items.

Sew-in hook-and-loop tape is suitable for a variety of different fabrics. It can be machine stitched to fabric using the straight stitch setting. Always close the tape together before laundering.

Stitching Velcro to fabric

DIY Repair Kit
- Velcro tape
- Scissors
- Needle
- Thread
- Pins
- Sewing machine (optional)

Step 1

Use a tape measure to determine what length of tape you require for the opening **A**. Cut two pieces of tape, 1 x hook and 1 x loop, to the same length.

Step 2

Position and then pin one piece of the tape to the fabric **B**

Step 3

Thread a needle with thread matching the colour of the tape. (*The step-by-step photos show contrasting thread being used, for clarity.*) Knot one end of the thread (see pages 16–17 for needle-threading and knotting techniques). Sew the tape to the fabric using straight stitch (see page 18) **C**. Try not to stitch all the way through to the other side of the fabric but instead catch just a few strands of fabric when sewing. When the stitching is completed, knot the thread securely and trim off with scissors **D**.

Step 4

Attach the second strip of tape in the same way ensuring that, once stitched, the two layers of tape will be aligned and will grip each other firmly, creating a neat closure **E**.

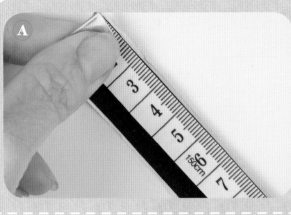

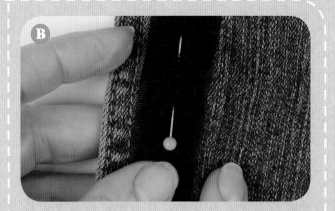

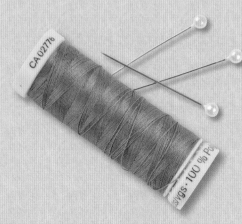

Ironing on Velcro closures

Iron-on Velcro tape is exactly the same as the sew-on variety (see pages 46-7), except that it has a pre-glued backing, which, when pressed down onto fabric and ironed, adheres to the fabric. It is suitable for use with cotton and linen fabrics, but is not suitable for use on synthetic, polyester, acrylic, wool or silk fabrics as the adhesive, when heated, may damage and distort the fabric.

Step 1
Carefully read the manufacturer's instructions on the package before using the tape. Position the smooth pre-glued side of one piece of the tape down onto the fabric **A**.

Step 2
Pin the tape in place so that it won't move when pressed with an iron **B**.

DIY Repair Kit

- Iron-on Velcro dots or strips
- Scissors
- Iron
- Handkerchief

Step 3
Turn the fabric over. Place a handkerchief over the fabric to prevent scorching. Set the iron to the correct heat setting as suggested by the packet instructions. Firmly press the iron onto the handkerchief. Hold the iron in place for several seconds **C**.

Step 4
Turn the fabric over and try to lift the edge of the tape with a fingernail. If it lifts, press it again until fully bonded to the fabric.

Step 5
Repeat this procedure for the opposite side, ensuring that the tape is placed in the correct position to align exactly with the tape on the other side of the closure. Once the second piece of tape is attached, wait five minutes before pressing the two layers together.

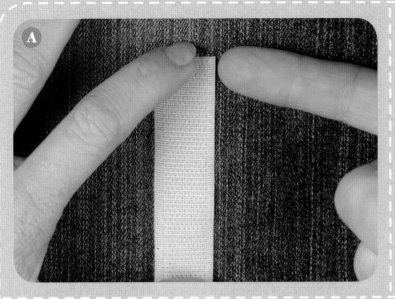

Savvy Sally says...

Never press the iron directly onto the tape as it will damage the surface.

Replacing metal snaps

Removing damaged snaps from a garment can be difficult and replacing them is not always that easy. Once the old or damaged snap is removed, it may be necessary to use a snap that is larger than the original so that the prongs of the new snap have some fabric to bite into.

Step 1

Using a butter knife slide the blade under the prongs of the snap **A** and pry them up out of the fibres of the fabric.

Step 2

Mark the place for the ball part of the snap on the overlap side of the garment with a fabric marker pen **B**. Read the directions on the packaging and follow the instructions for attaching the snap. You will probably need to use a snap tool **C**. The ball snap should now be secured neatly in place over the hole of the old ball snap **D**.

Step 3

Align the overlap of the closure and mark the place where the socket part of the fastener is to be positioned. Attach the socket part of the snap in the same way. You should now have both the ball and socket part of the snap attached to the garment **E**.

Practical Pete says...

Snaps come in a variety of different sizes. Keep a small collection in your DIY sewing kit for emergency situations. Keep them out of the reach of children as the prongs are very sharp and dangerous if swallowed.

A

B

C

D

E

DIY Repair Kit

- Packet of metal snaps
- Snap tool
- Butter knife

Replacing metal eyelets in fabric

Eyelets are usually made of a soft metal tube that is shaped by machine to look like a rivet. An eyelet is often used in casual clothing or garments that are secured with laces rather than buttons or zips. Designers insert them into garments to create a fashion statement. They can be both decorative and functional and come in a variety of different sizes and colours.

Savvy Sally says...

Use eyelet tools when working with lightweight fabrics and a hammer and punch with heavier materials.

If you wish to add a decorative finish to a ready-made garment using eyelets, visit your local craft shop. Coloured and fancy eyelets are often used by scrap book hobbyists. You'll find a wide selection on offer in the papercrafts section or online.

Step 1

If the eyelet in the fabric has been pulled out, patch the inside of the fabric before inserting a new one.

Step 2

Purchase an eyelet tool and pack of metal eyelets **A**. Carefully read the instructions on the packet before attempting to replace the eyelet.

Step 3

Mark the position for the eyelet with a water-soluble fabric marker. Cut a small X-shaped slit where the eyelet will be inserted. Carefully attach the eyelet blank to the lower jaw of the eyelet tool and a pronged eyelet to the upper jaw. Position the tool over your fabric, and squeeze it firmly **B**. You should now have a new eyelet in place **C**.

Alternatively...

Eyelet tools can be expensive. Check out craft shops for inexpensive tools used for papercrafts.

DIY Repair Kit

- Fabric for initial patching (if necessary)
- Water-soluble fabric marker
- Eyelet tool or hammer and punch
- Packet of eyelets

Attaching buttons and decorative studs to jeans

There are several stud kits on the market and you should read the instructions on the back of the packaging before commencing to attach the stud. These tools hold the stud in place over the outer garment and when they are hit with a hammer or pressed by hand, the jaws of the tool create enough pressure on the stud to force a hole in the fabric. This allows the stud to penetrate the fabric and seal with the backing tack on the inside of the garment. As the stud and its joining connector link, the metal is pressed together sealing the stud to the garment.

Step 1
Place both the stud and the backing tack **A** into the plastic applicator **B**.

Step 2
Using a fabric marker pen, mark the position for the new stud.

Step 3
Position the stud applicator around either side of the fabric, ensuring that the stud is on the outside of the fabric and the backing tack is on the inside **C**. Hit the applicator firmly with a hammer **D** to seal the stud **E**. If the fabric is very dense, or you are working with several layers of material, make a small hole with a darning needle to assist the securing of the back to the stud.

Practical Pete says...

Jean studs make a permanent hole in the fabric. Be sure of where you wish to attach the stud before fixing it to the material.

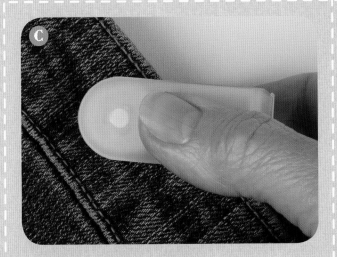

DIY Repair Kit

- Jean studs and applicator (kit)
- Fabric marker pen
- Hammer

Making holes in a leather belt

Most of us probably own a few trusted, good-quality leather belts that have become firm favourites to wear with trousers – whether casual jeans or formal business suits. But, over the years, most of us have also probably noticed our waistlines fluctuating! Whether you've been on a successful diet or gained a few pounds, it's very easy to punch in some new holes.

Step 1
Using a dressmaker's chalk pencil, mark on the inside of the belt where the desired hole is to be made **A**, making sure it is in the mid-line of the belt. To achieve a perfectly symmetrical and invisible finish you should ideally make any new holes the same distance apart as the existing holes on the belt (too many holes too close together may weaken the belt and cause it to twist). But if you are making just one extra hole, don't worry if it is a bit closer to any existing holes.

Step 2
Turn the head of the leather punch tool so that the correct size punch is sitting opposite the base of the pliers.

Step 3
Place the leather into the jaws of the punch tool. Place the tip of the punch over the mark for the new hole **B**.

Step 4
Grip the handles very firmly and squeeze tightly. A neat hole will be created. Remove the belt from the jaws **C**.

DIY Repair Kit
- Hole punch
- Dressmaking chalk

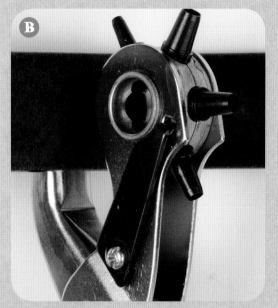

Alternatively...

If the leather is thick, make a small hole with a darning needle to help the jaws of the punch penetrate the belt.

Quick as a flash

Instant fixes

What do you do when you're at work and the hem of your dress or trouser comes down? If you have no sewing kit to hand and it really is a crisis, then you can reach for the office stapler. Another instant fix is double-sided sticky tape. Glue, safety pins, even bulldog clips, can have their uses. There are also many instant fixes that you can buy from the supermarket in your lunch hour.

The office stapler

While this tool can be a lifesaver, think twice before using it on silk or expensive garments as the staple may cut permanent holes into the fabric.

Step 1
To prevent the fabric from pinching up into an ugly pucker, place a thin layer of paper between the two folds of material. The paper will act as a stabilizer and give the stapler something to grip **A**. If it's a truly manic moment then forget about the paper and just staple the hem back into place.

Step 2
Then click, click, click ... and now you are fixed **B**.

Double-sided sticky tape

When buttons pop off or hems drop, double-sided sticky tape is so useful. It works especially well with light or semi-sheer fabrics, as it is thin and transparent. The steps below show how to fix a dropped hem.

Step 1
Cut the desired length of tape with scissors. Position the tape and press the sticky side down onto the inside of the fabric **A**.

Step 2
Peel off the backing paper to expose the other pre-glued side **B**.

Step 3
Fold the hem back over and press the edge down onto the tape. Press from the middle outwards towards each end of the tape **C**.

Step 4
As you can see, there are no marks or holes, and the hem has been instantly (albeit temporarily) fixed **D**.

Safety pins

The nifty safety pin can get you out of most over-exposure situations. If your blouse is gaping, slip a small gold safety pin through the inside facing on the garment, catching a small section of the top layer of fabric. Fasten the pin closed. At a later date, attach a small snap to secure the opening more securely. If the hem of trousers or a skirt has come down then quickly press it into position and fix it to the inside of the garment with several small pins.

The office stapler

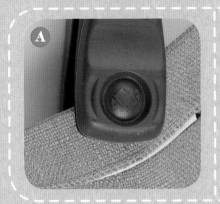

Double-sided sticky tape

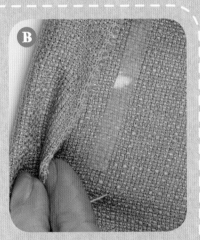

Savvy Sally says...

Remove the tape and stitch the hem back into place before laundering the garment.

Fabric glue

Fabric glue is available at most craft and haberdashery shops. There are several different types on the market and they can be very handy for instant repairs to a wide variety of garments and fabrics. Always read the instructions on the packet or bottle to check whether it can be used on the material you need to repair, particularly leather.

Gluing on a leather patch

Getting leather repaired can be very expensive, but to do it yourself can be difficult. If a leather garment is torn then it's advisable to have it professionally repaired, but if the garment is very old or this is not financially viable then a patch glued over the tear may solve the problem. Ready-made leather patches in a variety of colours can be found in good haberdashery stores. Alternatively, embroidered motifs can add a designer look to some leather jackets, if the repair is in a suitable place, at the top of a sleeve or on a breast pocket.

Step 1

Lay the leather garment face up . Apply a small amount of glue over the back of the patch, which needs to be sufficiently larger than the hole or tear in order to adhere to the leather around it.

Step 2

Wait until the glue becomes tacky and then press the patch over the top of the tear.

Gluing up a leather hem

If the hem of a leather skirt or jacket needs repairing then fabric glue will do the job quickly and efficiently. Using a small paint brush apply a thin layer of glue onto the inside of the hem, wait until the glue becomes tacky and then press the two layers of leather together. Leave the glue to dry for a few hours before wearing the garment.

Bulldog clips

If the buttons pop off a knitted cardigan, reach into the office drawer for a bulldog clip. It may look a little unusual, but it could be a good topic of conversation with that cute guy who keeps popping by your desk for a quick chat.

Brooches

Brooches are perfect for an instant fix. They can be used as a decorative replacement for buttons, hooks and clasps. Keep a couple of spare brooches of different sizes in your instant DIY repair kit.

Iron-on patches

Iron-on patches can be bought from the fabric sections of all good department stores and haberdashery shops, and are available in plain colours or as embroidered motifs. The back of the patch is impregnated with heat-sensitive glue, which, when activated by the iron, adheres to fabric. It is important to read the application instructions before pressing the patch onto the garment.

Step 1

Purchase a patch in the same type of fabric as the garment you wish to repair, and in a matching colour (in the step-by-step photos a contrasting patch is shown for clarity). Set the iron to the recommended heat setting for the fabric. Turn the garment inside out.

Step 2

Place the glue side of the patch over the tear. Cover the patch with a handkerchief. Press the iron over the covered patch and hold in place for several seconds.

Step 3

Check to see if the glue has melted sufficiently by trying to lift one corner of the patch. If it's not completely attached, iron the patch again. Allow the patch to cool before wearing the garment.

Fabric glue

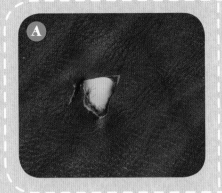 **A**

 **B**

 **C**

Bulldog clips

Iron-on patches

 **A**

 **B**

 **C**

 **D**

Brooches

Iron-on decorative motifs

Iron-on decorative motifs come in a huge range of shapes and designs, and often have additional embellishments **A**. Like plain, iron-on patches, they have heat-activated adhesive on the back **B**. They can be used to cover tears, holes and permanent stains and are applied like iron-on patches (see page 62), except that they are pressed onto the right side of the material; not the inside, where they would be concealed **C**.

If the motif you use is embellished with sequins or beads, you will need to place a handkerchief over the top of the motif before ironing to prevent them being damaged **D**. Crystal-embedded motifs can also be used.

Making your own decorative motif

Creating your own decorative motif is easy – all you need is a suitable piece of fabric or lace **A** and some heat-sensitive bonding web.

Bonding web is available in craft and haberdashery shops. It seals the edges of fabric so that it won't fray once bonded to a garment. Ask for webbing that has a paper backing, as it is easier to use **B**.

Step 1

Cut a piece of webbing large enough to cover the fabric you wish to use as a motif. Place the webbing-side down onto the wrong side of the material. Press the paper backing with a warm dry iron. Constantly move the iron over the paper to prevent scorching the fabric **C**.

Step 2

Once fused, peel away the paper, trim the webbing to match the shape of the fabric or lace and iron it onto your garment just as you would with a ready-made decorative motif (see above).

Press-stick Velcro

Velcro press-stick dots **A** and strips **B** are great for emergency repairs. Most supermarkets have a small stand stocked with haberdashery items. Pop a small packet into your desk drawer or the glove compartment of your car. These handy items can be used as an instant fix for a broken zip.

Step 1

Select the tape and dots you need, cutting the tape to the required length, peel off the backing paper of the rough 'hook' side of the Velcro and stick down firmly onto one side of the closure **C**.

Step 2

Apply the soft 'loop' side of the Velcro onto the other side of the closure, ensuring that they are aligned to overlap neatly **D**.

The use of press-stick Velcro is very much a temporary measure as the adhesive is not nearly as strong as sew-in Velcro (see pages 46–7) or iron-on Velcro (see pages 48–9). Rather than test the permanency of this repair, it is best to change clothes at the earliest opportunity.

Practical Pete says...

Remove the tape and replace the zip before laundering the garment.

Iron-on decorative motifs

Press-stick Velcro

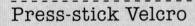

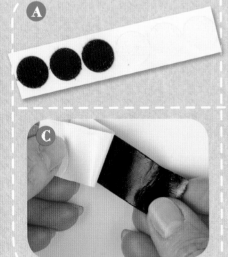

Make your own

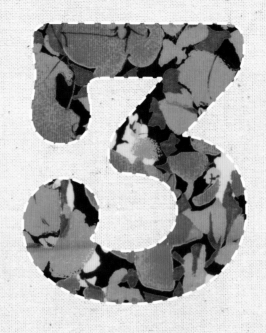

Zip it

D

F

Replacing a centred zip

A centred zip is usually sewn into the back seam of a garment. The back seam is stitched closed from the end of the zipper through to the hem of the garment. The open seam that is left unstitched is pressed flat along the stitching line. The teeth of the zip are centred between the folds of the fabric. Once the zip is inserted into the fabric and stitched in place, the zip closes the seam forming a neat and centred closure.

Step 1
Depending on whether the zip is in a skirt, dress, blouse or trouser, if it needs to be replaced, the stitching that attaches the waistband or neck facing will need to be unpicked to allow access for removal and replacement of the zip. Use a seam ripper to undo just a small amount of stitching, sufficient to be able to remove the broken zip **A**

Step 2
Place the closed zip face up under one edge of the folded seam. Move the fold of the fabric so that it is centred over the zip. Pin the zip tape in place to prevent it from slipping when stitched **B**

Step 3
Draw a stitching line of the fabric with the fabric marker **C**. Thread the sewing machine with matching thread. Attach the zip foot and set the sewing machine to straight stitch with a stitch length of 1.5mm and sew down the stitching line marked on the fabric **D**. Back-stitch at the end to fasten off and remove the fabric from the machine.

Step 4
Pin the other side of the zip tape to the opposite side of the seam opening and mark a stitching line on the fabric line with a fabric marker. Stitch it in place using the same method as described in step 3 **D**. Back stitch at the end to fasten off, remove the fabric from the machine and trim the excess thread with scissors **E**. To finish, take the metal toggle and zip the teeth up to the top of the zip closing the open seam **F**, and slip stitch (see page 20) the facings or waistband back into position.

DIY Repair Kit
- Seam ripper
- Embroidery scissors
- Replacement zip
- Needle
- Thread
- Pins
- Fabric marker pen
- Ruler
- Sewing machine with zip foot

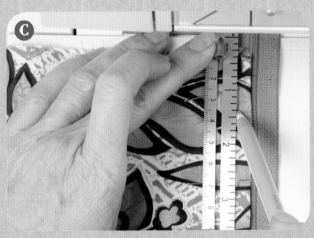

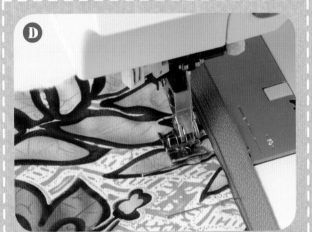

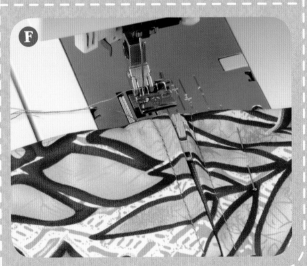

Replacing a lapped zip

A lapped zipper is used in the back or side seam of skirts, trousers or dresses. Usually the left-hand seam of the zipper fabric is folded and stitched so that the teeth of the zip are concealed under the fold of the fabric. This is a very neat form of zipper insertion.

Step 1
Unpick the facings or waistband stitching using a seam ripper or the point of embroidery scissors so that you can access the broken zip. Remove the old zip by carefully unpicking the stitches.

Step 2
Position the closed zip face up under the left fold of the seam opening. Place the zip stop ¾in (1.5cm) below the stitching line for the waistband or facings **A**. Using a fabric marker pen and ruler, mark stitching lines on the fabric down the left side of the closure **B**.

Step 3
Tack the zip into place with big, loose, straight stitches or pin it into place to prevent the zip from moving when being machine-stitched **C**.

Step 4
Attach the zip foot to the sewing machine and set the machine for straight stitch with a stitch length of 2.5mm. Sew close to the edge of the seam **D**. To secure the stitching when you reach the end of the garment opening, press the back stitch button and stitch backwards over two or three of the stitches previously made. Remove the fabric from the machine and snip the excess thread with scissors.

Step 5
Lap the front opening edge of the seam over the left back edge matching the seam line. The front will lap approximately ⅛in (3mm) over the zip, covering the zip teeth.

Step 6
Mark the stitching line with a fabric marker pen if you are concerned that you may not sew straight. Sew down the stitching line and pivot at the end of the opening. Sew across the fabric to seal the end of the zip. Remove the fabric from the machine and trim off the excess threads **E**.

DIY Repair Kit
- Replacement zip
- Thread
- Needle
- Seam ripper
- Scissors
- Fabric marker pen
- Ruler
- Pins
- Sewing machine with zip foot

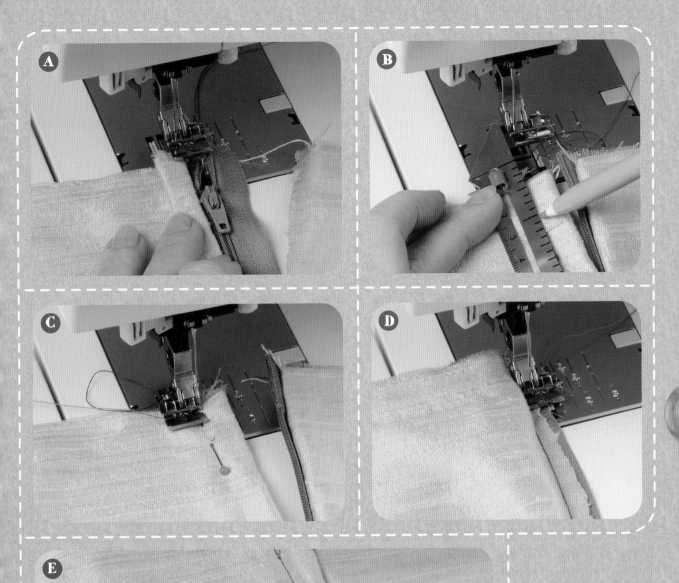

Replacing a trouser zip

A trouser zip can be the most complicated thing to replace in a garment. If you have never sewn before, ask for help from an experienced sewer before attempting to replace one yourself in a quality pair of trousers. It may well be worth paying your dry cleaners to replace the zip professionally. For those with some sewing knowledge and who can operate a sewing machine, then this technique will show you how to replace a front fly zip.

Step 1
Carefully unpick the waistband at the top of the zip on both sides of the trouser waistband to release the zip and the zip fly facings **A**.

Step 2
Carefully unpick the front fly facings that conceal the edges of the zip. Note how they were attached and if necessary draw a little diagram to remind yourself how they should be reattached to the zip **B**.

Step 3
Pin or tack the zip into place with big, loose, straight stitches, face side up on the front fly facing **C**. Ensure that the base stop of the zip sits ¼in (6mm) below where the zip pull will finish once sewn in.

Step 4
Thread the sewing machine and attach the zip foot. Stitch from the top of the zip down to the end of the facing **D**. Back-stitch to secure the thread before removing the garment from the machine. Snip the threads off close to the last stitches with scissors.

Step 5
Pin and then carefully stitch the opposite side of the zip between the under-fly facing and the seam of the garment. Stitch from the top of the zip down to the end of the fly facing, encasing the zip between the two layers of fabric.

Step 6
Mark a stitching line for the fly front on top of the original stitching holes, using a water-soluble pen or white dressmaking chalk **E**.

Step 7
On the outside of the garment, sew from the waistband down the stitching line of the front fly, catching the under-facing as you stitch, and across the bottom end of the zip **F**.

Remove the garment from the machine and trim off the ends of the threads. On the inside of the garment secure the two layers of the facings together at the base of the fly **G**.

Step 8
Slip-stitch the waistband back into position **H** so that it is covering the fly facings and ends of the zip **I**.

DIY Repair Kit
- Replacement zip
- Thread
- Needle
- Sewing machine with zip foot
- Scissors
- Dressmaking chalk
- Water-soluble pen
- Pins

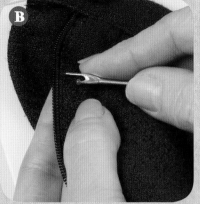

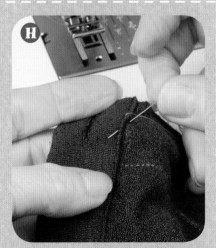

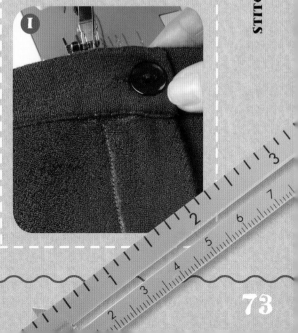

Replacing a concealed zip

Replacing a concealed zip can be tricky because the zip teeth are concealed on the inside of the zip tape; sewing experience is necessary. Once zipped up, the zip is almost invisible as it joins the two seams of a garment flush together. Concealed zips are fairly fragile and should not be used in garments that are particularly tight, as they are prone to break under stress.

To insert a concealed zip, the zip needs to be unzipped. The zip tape also needs to be at least 1in (2.5cm) longer than the seam opening because it is impossible to stitch to the stopper at the base of the zip.

Step 1
Unpick the waistband or the facings at the top of the zip to gain access. Unpick the zip from the seams of the garment **A**. The seam will need to be unpicked about 2in (5cm) below where the zip ended **B**.

Step 2
Unzip the zip and place one tape right-side down against the stitching seam on the garment. Tack or pin the tape in place to prevent it from moving when being stitched. As you can see in this illustration, the teeth of the green zip actually roll slightly in towards the zip tape. When you are stitching a zip into place gently press the teeth out flat as you sew **C**

Step 3
Attach the concealed zip foot and move the needle position on your machine so that you are able to

Savvy Sally says...

Never press a concealed zip with an iron, as it will permanently damage the zip making it inoperable.

sew close up to the zip teeth but not right up against them. It is important that the zip toggle can slide down the zip and not get caught in the stitching **D**. Sew down the edge of the zip teeth to within 1in (2.5cm) of the end of the tape. Back-stitch to secure the thread and remove from the machine. Snip off the excess threads closely.

Step 4
Repeat step 2 on the other side of the zip by facing it down along the seam allowance of the garment. Pin it in place and try zipping up the opening to check it you have pinned it on correctly **E**. Change the needle position on the sewing machine so that the needle sits close to the zip teeth. Stitch from the top of the zip down towards the end of the tape, finishing 1in (2.5cm) before the end of the zip.

Step 5
Machine- or slip-stitch the side seam and waistband or facings back into position.

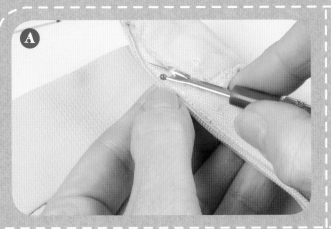

A

B

C

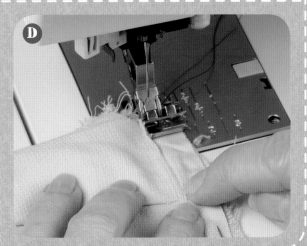

D

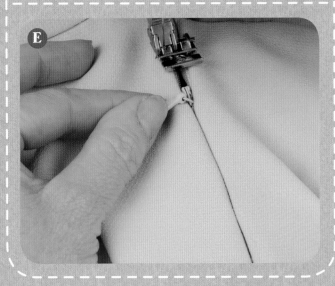

E

DIY Repair Kit

- Replacement zip
- Sewing machine with concealed zip foot
- Needle
- Thread
- Scissors
- Pins
- Seam ripper

4

Seams simple

Mending a seam with back stitch

Often the seams on skirts or trousers weaken over a period of time due to stress on that section of stitching. When threads break and stitches unravel, thread a needle and repair it quickly and easily using this strong and easy-to-master stitch. Always practise on a scrap of fabric if you haven't sewn before. Once your stitches are neat and regular, you're ready to make the DIY repair.

Step 1
Seams can weaken and come open on any garment **A**. Pin the open seam together. Thread a needle with thread to match your garment. Tie a double knot joining the two ends together. Make a neat stitch in the fabric to secure the thread **B**.

Step 2
Make a small straight stitch. Make a second stitch and as the needle comes up and out of the fabric, pass the point of the needle down the exit hole of the first stitch **C**

Step 3
Make another stitch keeping the spacing of the stitches even. Back-stitch into the exit of the second stitch. Continue sewing until the seam is repaired. Knot off the thread and trim off any excess thread **D**

Step 4
Press the mended seam flat with a warm iron and pressing cloth **E**.

DIY Repair Kit
- Needle
- Thread
- Scissors
- Pins
- Iron

Savvy Sally says...

Keep a basket for garments that need repairing in the laundry. Once a month, set aside an evening to sew up seams or replace buttons. If done regularly, DIY mending needn't seem like a never-ending chore.

A

B

C

D

E

Taking in a seam

Have you been on a successful diet and now all your clothes are too big?
Or is a staple piece of your wardrobe just a bit loose in a certain place?
Not all such clothes need to go to the charity shop, especially those favourite
or designer pieces that you know you look fabulous in. Instead, you can simply
take in a few seams and extend their lifespan.

Step 1
Turn the garment inside out and put it on. Pinch the excess fabric with one hand and pin it (it can be helpful to have someone else do this for you). Carefully remove the garment and then straighten up the pins, adding a few more if necessary **A**.

Step 2
Turn the garment right side out and try it on again to double check that the alteration is correct and not too tight or still too loose – adjust the pins if necessary. Turn the garment inside out once more and mark a stitching line with a fabric marker pen, following the placement of the pins **B**.

Step 3
If sewing by hand, thread a needle with thread matching the colour of the garment. Knot one end of the thread (see pages 16–17 for needle-threading and knotting techniques). Sew down the new seam line using small, neat back stitches (see page 22). If using a sewing machine, set it on straight stitch with a stitch length of 1.5mm, and sew along the marked line, removing the pins as you go **C**. Back-stitch when you start and finish to secure the thread. Knot off the threads when the stitching is completed and trim off the excess threads with scissors.

Step 4
Press the new seam with a warm iron. If the fabric is particularly bulky open up the old seam with embroidery scissors or a seam ripper, and iron between the two flaps of fabric so that they can lie flat. Alternatively – if you're confident you won't need to let the garment out again – you could trim off some of the now-increased seam allowance, but be careful to still leave a seam allowance of at least ½in (1cm). Turn the garment right side out and iron the new seam again, placing a clean handkerchief between the iron and the garment to help protect delicate fabrics from scorching **D**.

DIY Repair Kit
- Pins
- Needle
- Thread
- Scissors
- Fabric marker pen
- Sewing machine (if using)
- Iron and pressing cloth

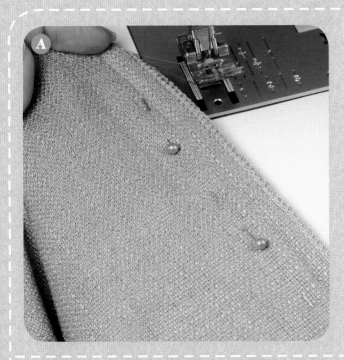

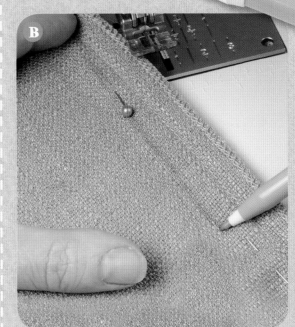

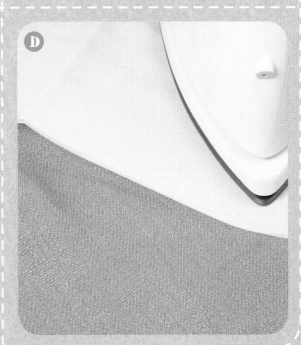

Letting out a seam

Letting out a seam is not a big deal as long as there is sufficient fabric inside the stitched seam to let out! Some ready-made garments have been stitched together with an overlocker sewing machine, which cuts off the seam allowance, overcasts the raw edges and stitches the seam together all at the same time. If a garment has no seam allowance, then it's time to pass it on to a friend or charity shop, as trying to make it larger is too time-consuming.

Step 1
Turn the garment inside out. With a water-soluble marker pen, mark on the seam line where you wish to let out the seam **A**.

Step 2
Unpick the seam with a seam ripper or the point of embroidery scissors **B** and **C**.

Step 3
If sewing by hand, thread a needle with thread matching the colour of the garment. Knot one end of the thread (see pages 16–17 for needle-threading and knotting techniques). Stitch the new seam together using small, neat back stitches (see page 22). If using a sewing machine, set it on straight stitch with a stitch length of 1.5mm, and sew along the marked line **D**. When you have completed the stitching fasten off the threads and trim them down close to the last few stitches with scissors.

Step 4
With the garment still inside out, slightly dampen the seam with a mist of water or place a damp handkerchief over the seam allowance. Press the fabric with a warm dry iron **E** to remove the old stitching marks and to open out the seam.

DIY Repair Kit
- Fabric marker
- Ruler
- Seam ripper
- Needle and thread or sewing machine
- Scissors
- Iron and pressing cloth

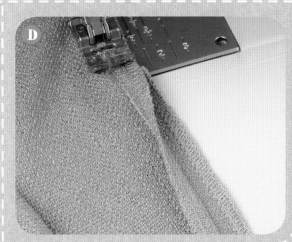

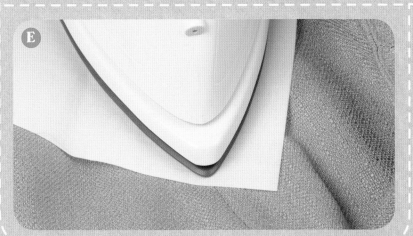

Repairing a split seam in the crotch of trousers

The seams in the crotch of trousers often split simply through the friction of daily wear and tear or because they were originally sewn with a poor-quality thread. But don't worry, this is easy to repair by hand or machine, so you can keep those favourite old trousers going a good while longer.

Step 1

Seams in the crotch of trousers are often the first to wear out **A**. Turn the trousers inside out and pin the split seam of the crotch together **B**. If sewing by hand, thread a needle with thread similar in colour to the fabric of the garment. (*The step-by-step photos show contrasting thread being used, for clarity.*) Knot the two strands of thread together (see pages 16–17 for needle-threading and knotting techniques). If using a sewing machine, set it on straight stitch with a stitch length of 1.5mm.

Step 2

Secure the thread at the end of the split seam. Back-stitch over at least 1in (2.5cm) of the machine stitching before the split **C**. Now sew along the original stitching line in back stitch (see page 22) using small, neat, even stitches.

Step 3

Stitch past the split and continue to sew along the machine stitching on the trouser seam for a further 1in (2.5cm) before knotting off the thread **D**. Snip off the excess threads with scissors.

Step 4

To reinforce the seam of the crotch, cut a length of bias binding and pin it over the repair **E**.

Step 5

Sew the bias binding over the crotch seam **F**. If you are sewing by hand use straight stitch. Use a narrow zigzag stitch if sewing by machine. Set the machine stitch width to 1.5mm and the stitch length to 2mm.

DIY Repair Kit
- Needle and thread or sewing machine
- Pins
- Scissors
- Bias binding

SEAMS SIMPLE

STITCH 'N' FIX

Repairing a split seam in stretch fabric

Stretch fabric is very different from woven fabric. It has a completely different weave and is made from either synthetic or natural fibres mixed with Lycra or spandex so that, once woven together, the fabric stretches. Just how much the stitches will stretch is determined by how wide the stitches are and the distance between them.

Stretch fabric is often used in leisure and fitness clothing, and as such the seams are often put under extra movement and strain. Thus it is a common problem for the seams in your jogging pants, for example, to split open **A**.

Sewing stretch fabric by hand

Step 1
Thread a needle with polyester thread similar in colour to the fabric of the garment. (*The step-by-step photos show contrasting thread being used, for clarity.*) Knot the two strands of thread together.

Step 2
Back-stitch to start, commencing to stitch along the original machine stitching 1in (2.5cm) before the split occurs. Sew neat little zigzag stitches (see page 24), keeping them evenly spaced and fairly close together **B**

Stitch past the split and back over another 1in (2.5cm) of machine stitching before knotting the thread and snipping it off with scissors.

Sewing stretch fabric by machine

Step 1
Set the sewing machine to zigzag, with a stitch length of approximately 1.5mm and a stitch width of 2mm. Back-stitch over a small section of stitches before the split and continue to sew along the original stitching line, sewing the seam back together **C**, and continue another 1in (2.5cm) past the end of the split.

Step 2
Back-stitch to secure the thread at the end of your sewing. Remove the garment from the machine and trim off the excess threads with scissors.

A

B

C

DIY Repair Kit
- Needle
- Matching thread
- Sewing machine (optional)
- Scissors

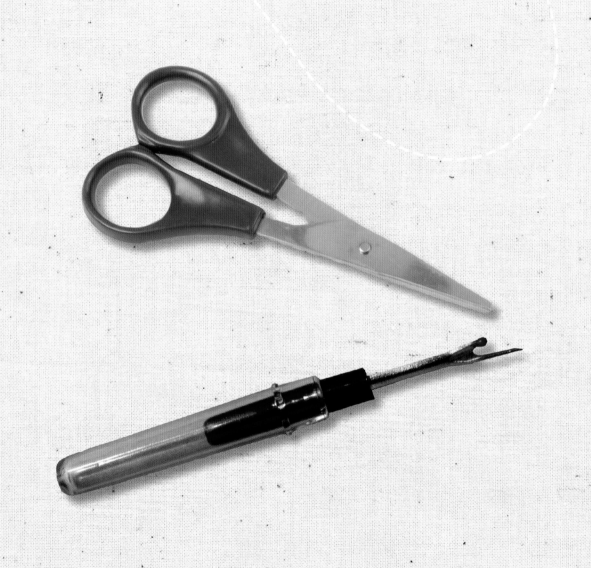

Hemmed in

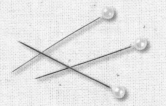

Using iron-on hemming web

You don't even need to learn how to sew in order to fix a hem. Hemming tape or web is sold in supermarkets and craft shops and comes in a variety of different widths. The web is a fine layer of heat-sensitive glue. When placed between two layers of material and heated with an iron the web melts, sticking the two layers of fabric together.

Practical Pete says...

Ironing the repaired hem through a handkerchief or cloth will help to prevent scorching, and if any webbing becomes dislodged it will stick to the hanky, not the iron. If the web does come into direct contact with the face of the iron it will melt on to it and you'll have a sticky black mess that's difficult to get off!

Step 1
Measure the length of hem that needs to be repaired using a tape measure **A**.

Step 2
Cut the required length of hemming web **B**.

Step 3
Slide the web under the free edge of the hem and position it so that it is concealed by the fabric **C**.

Step 4
Place a slightly damp handkerchief or clean piece of fabric over the hem and press with a warm iron **D**. Allow the hem to cool completely before wearing or laundering the garment.

A

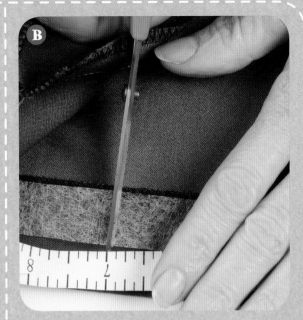

B

C

D

DIY Repair Kit

- Roll of hemming web
- Scissors
- Iron
- Handkerchief or pressing cloth
- Tape measure

Repairing a hem with herringbone stitch

Herringbone stitch is the ideal stitch for repairing the hem on a skirt or trousers. It may take a little longer to sew than the simple slip stitch (see page 20), but it creates a secure neat finish that is well worth the effort when mending quality clothing. Before starting your repair, you may wish to practise the stitch by reviewing the step-by-step technique demonstrated on page 22.

Step 1
Carefully secure the threads of the unravelled hem. Thread a needle and back-stitch (see page 22) the threads to the edge of the hem to secure them in place. Trim off any excess thread with scissors.

Step 2
Pin the unravelled hem in place **A**. Thread a needle and tie a knot in one end of the thread. Back-stitch into the hem edge to secure the thread **B**.

Step 3
Make a long, diagonal stitch from left to right across the free edge of the hem fold and back through the flat fabric of the garment, about ¼in (6mm) from the hem edge **C**.

Step 4
With the needle pointing to the left, make a small stitch in the fabric. Pierce the fabric with the point of the needle sewing from right to left **D**.

Step 5
Bring the needle out of the hem and make another long, diagonal stitch from left to right so that the threads cross **E**. The stitches should be evenly spaced and approximately the same size **F**.

Step 6
When the stitching is complete, finish off by back- stitching in the edge of the folded hem fabric before cutting the excess thread with scissors.

DIY Repair Kit
- Pins
- Needle
- Matching thread
- Scissors

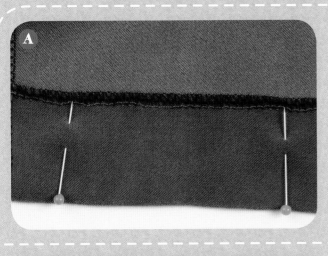

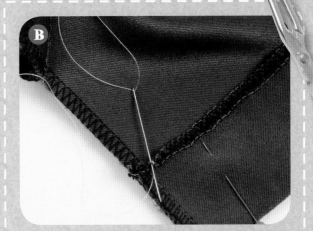

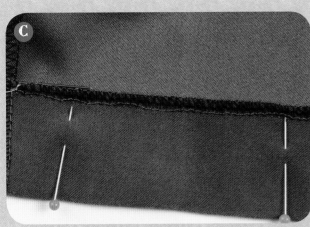

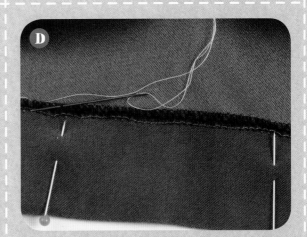

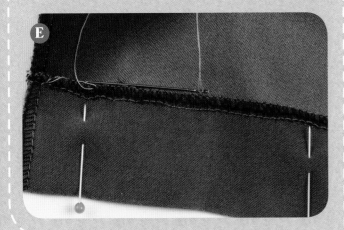

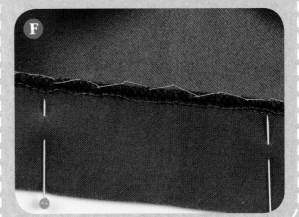

Invisible hems using transparent thread and interfacing

This is a particularly handy technique for hemming fabric such as silk or linen where you wish the hemming stitches to be as unobtrusive on the right side of the fabric as possible. In the step-by-step photographs, right, a contrasting pink thread has been used, as opposed to transparent thread, for clarity.

Step 1

Measure and cut out a piece of interfacing to the width and length of the hem to be repaired. Mark the outline of the piece with a fabric marker pen if this helps **A**

DIY Repair Kit

- Tape measure
- Interfacing
- Fabric marker pen (optional)
- Iron
- Handkerchief or pressing cloth
- Fine needle
- Transparent nylon thread

Step 2

Place the piece of interfacing over the opened-up area of hem (i.e. onto the wrong side of the fabric) **B**. Place a handkerchief or clean piece of fabric over the top and press, working along the very edge of the fabric of the hem.

Step 3

Measure the depth of the intended hem and pin the hem up into position **C**. Press the fold of the hem lightly with an iron **D**

Step 4

Using transparent thread, sew the folded edge of the hem to the flat interfaced fabric of the garment using slip stitch (see page 20) or herringbone stitch (see page 22 and photo **E**). Knot off the ends of the thread securely when the sewing is completed.

Savvy Sally says...

Never place a hot iron directly over transparent threads as they may melt. Always cover the seam or hem with a cloth before pressing.

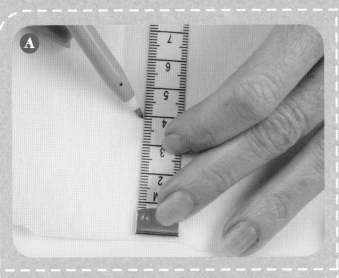

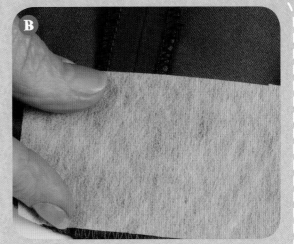

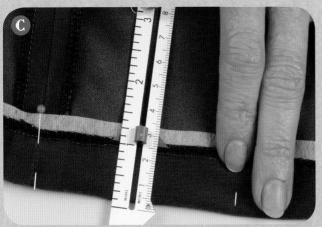

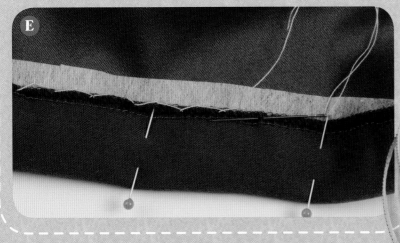

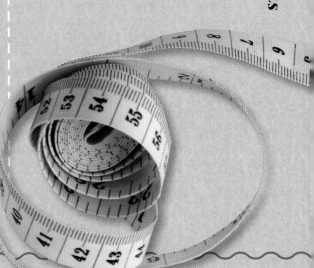

Hemming with slip stitch

Slip stitch is a fast, easy stitch to master and is ideal for quickly repairing or taking up hems on clothing, curtains and many other home furnishings. Before commencing your repair, you may wish to practise doing slip stitch by reviewing the step-by-step technique demonstrated on page 20.

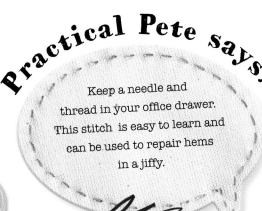

Practical Pete says...

Keep a needle and thread in your office drawer. This stitch is easy to learn and can be used to repair hems in a jiffy.

Step 1
Secure the threads of the unravelled hem. Thread a needle and back-stitch (see page 22) the threads to the edge of the hem to secure them in place. Trim off any excess thread with scissors. Pin the hem to be stitched in place **A**.

Step 2
Work from right to left. Thread a needle with a long strand of thread that is colour-matched to the fabric. (*The step-by-step photos show contrasting thread being used, for clarity.*) Knot only one end of the thread. Make a little back stitch in the edge of the hem to secure the knot **B**.

Step 3
With the very tip of the needle pick up a few threads of the inside of the garment (i.e. not the hem itself) just level with the edge of the hem **C**.

Step 4
Pull the needle until all the thread has been pulled through the strands of fabric.

Step 5
Slide the needle into the edge of the hem making a small stitch. Slide it along and bring it up and out of the hem close to the edge of the hem fabric **D**.

Step 6
Repeat steps 3–5 and continue to stitch **E** until you reach the original stitching. Back-stitch over the original stitching to secure the thread and trim off the excess with scissors.

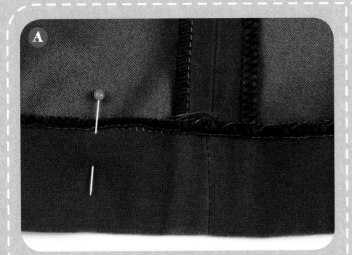

A

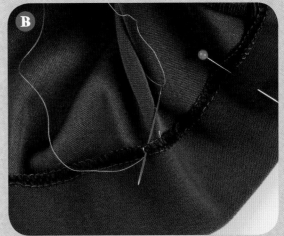

B

C

D

E

DIY Repair Kit

- Pins
- Needle
- Matching thread
- Scissors

Repairing frayed trouser-leg hems

Cotton trousers and jeans fray at the base of the hem because they are either too long and drag on the ground when one walks or they wear out from constantly rubbing on the back of the heels of shoes. It's not hard to repair the frayed hems but it is advisable to do so before they are beyond repair. If left too long it's almost impossible to do. This technique will shorten the trouser length.

Step 1
The base of trouser hems can become worn and frayed **Ⓐ**. Unpick the original stitching on the hem **Ⓑ**.

Step 2
Press the hem fabric with a warm iron.

Step 3
Measure the circumference and depth of the hem **Ⓒ**. Transfer these measurements onto some iron-on interfacing and cut two lengths of interfacing to the desired length and width – one to be ironed into the inside of the trouser leg, the other around the inside of the hem. If you are repairing *both* trouser legs, you will need four pieces of interfacing, two for each leg. Ensure when repairing both trouser legs that the hems measure the same width and length, both before and after repair.

Step 4
Cut the hem from the trouser leg with scissors, as close to the frayed edge as possible. Cut both lengths of interfacing down the centre, thus cutting them to half the depth measurement. With an iron, press one strip of the interfacing onto the inside of the cut-off hem **Ⓓ** and the other onto the inside trouser leg material where the hem will be reattached **Ⓔ**.

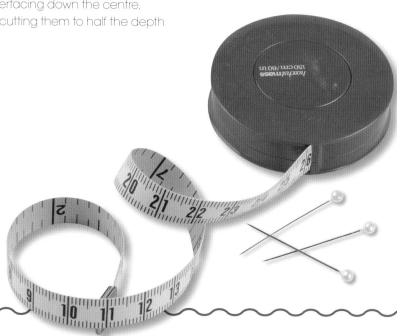

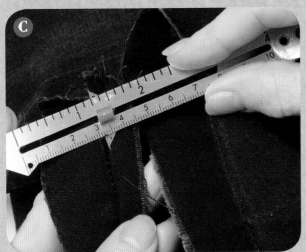

Step 5

Pin the hem fabric back to the trouser leg with right side of fabrics together **F**. Using thread to match the colour of the trousers, back-stitch (by hand) or straight-stitch (by machine) the trouser hem back onto the lower edge of the trouser leg **G**. Keep the stitches very small and neat. The interfacing will reinforce the hem fabric, which will help to prevent further fraying.

Step 6

Fold the hem back over to conceal the interfacing **H** and pin it into place ready to be stitched **I**.

Step 7

Finally, stitch the hem in place, using a slip stitch or machine straight stitch **J**.

Step 8

You will then have a finished trouser hem with no more fraying **K**. Snip off any remaining tails of thread **L**.

Savvy Sally says...

The hems on trousers and seams usually fray because they're too long. To prevent them from fraying, take up the hem before wearing them and you won't need to make any further repairs in the future.

DIY Repair Kit

- Iron-on interfacing
- Iron
- Needle
- Matching thread
- Scissors
- Seam ripper
- Pins
- Tape measure
- Sewing machine (optional)

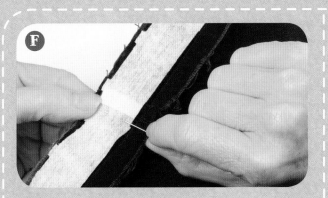

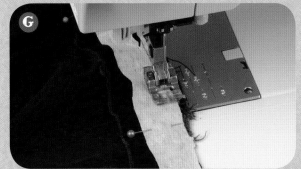

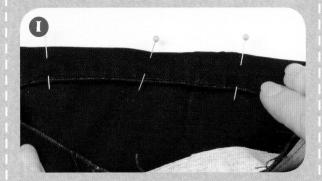

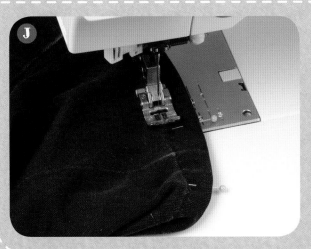

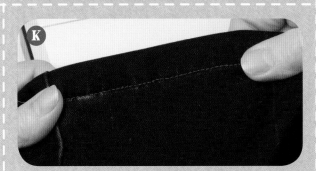

Machine-stitching a hem using top stitch

Top stitching is used on denim to finish the hems and to add designer detail to the seams. It is also used as a decorative finish in tailoring and for high street fashions. Top-stitching thread is heavier and thicker than regular sewing threads. It is usually a different colour to the fabric as the stitches are intended to be visible.

To prevent the thread from fraying as it feeds through the metal eye of the needle and into the fabric, it is important that the correct needle is used. A jeans needle, size 100, will stitch most top-stitching threads.

Step 1

Top stitching can also be used decoratively and uses a heavier thread than normal **B**. Thread the machine with top-stitching thread **C** and set the machine for straight stitch. If there is a top-stitching pattern included in your machine's stitch memory, then selecting this will ensure that the machine sews the desired stitch.

Step 2

Pin the hem or seam of the fabric you wish to topstitch. Mark a sewing line with a fabric marker **D**.

Step 3

Sew on the right side of the fabric **E**, as this is the visible side **F**.

Step 4

When the stitching is completed, back-stitch over a few stitches to secure the thread, remove the fabric from the machine, and trim off the cotton end **G**. Press the stitching with a warm iron.

DIY Repair Kit

- Sewing machine
- Jeans needle
- Top-stitching thread
- Pins
- Scissors
- Water-soluble marker pen

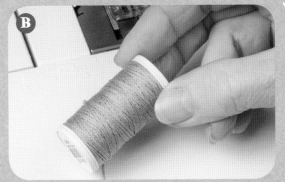

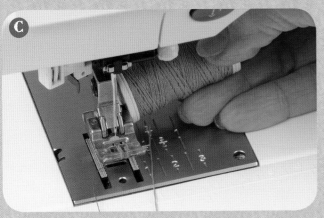

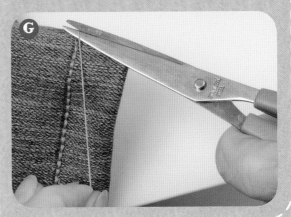

Machine-stitching a hem using blind stitch

A blind stitch hem is ideal for medium-to-heavyweight fabrics. Most modern sewing machines have this stitch built into their stitch memory. It consists of several small straight stitches followed by one zigzag stitch that jumps to the left. The jump stitch catches the fold of the hem fabric as the machine sews.

Step 1
Fold the hem up to the desired depth. Fold the hem back on itself approximately ¼in (6mm) so that the finished edge of the hem is to the right of the fold. Pin in place **A**.

Step 2
If you have the sewing machine manual for your machine read the instructions before starting to sew. Attach the blind hem foot and thread the machine with matching thread or transparent thread. (*The step-by-step photos show contrasting thread being used, for clarity.*)

Step 3
As you stitch, the metal guard on the foot should run parallel with the fold of the fabric **B**. The straight stitch will sew onto the finished edge of the hem and the jump stitch will catch a few fibres of the fold **C**. Back-stitch to secure the threads when finished.

Step 4
When the stitching is completed remove the fabric from the machine. Trim off the excess thread. Turn the fabric right side over **D** and place a handkerchief or pressing cloth over the stitches but not over the folded edge of the hem. Press the stitches with a warm iron. Do not press the fold of the hem if you are sewing a garment as a blind hem should roll softly and have a rounded finish.

DIY Repair Kit
- Sewing machine and blind hemming foot
- Transparent thread
- Iron
- Handkerchief or pressing cloth
- Pins

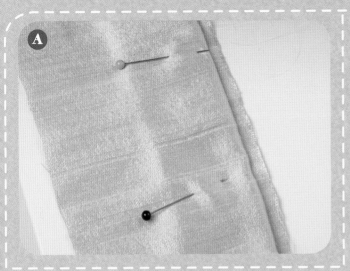

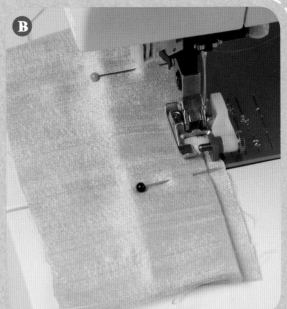

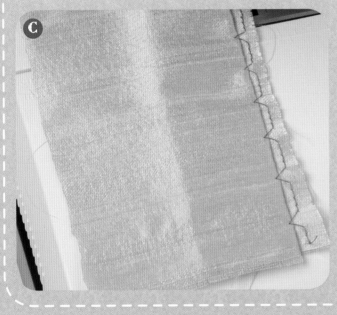

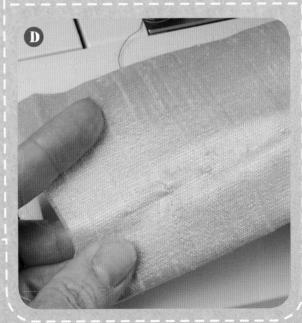

Making a jumped hem on a lined skirt

This is a couture technique often used on lined garments, such as ballgowns or wedding gowns. However, if you have a lined, ready-made skirt from which you wish to remove any trace of stitching at the hemline then it is possible to sew the free edge of the hem to the lining fabric so that no stitching is seen on the hem of the outer garment. This is ideal when working with heavyweight silks on which, no matter how carefully you sew, the stitching shows on the outer fabric.

Step 1
Unpick about 12in (23cm) of a side seam in the lining fabric **A**.

Step 2
Carefully unpick the hem with a seam ripper or needle **B**.

Step 3
Turn the garment inside out so that the right side of the lining hem and of the garment hem are touching.

Step 4
Stitch the edges of the hems together, sewing all around the hem and back-stitching to secure the threads **C**.

Step 5
Turn the garment right side out through the opening made in the side seam of the lining. Slip-stitch the opening in the lining closed **D**.

Step 6
Press the inside of the garment where the two hems have been joined **E**. Place a pressing cloth over the fold in the hem and press gently with a warm iron. The stitches will be invisible from the outside of the garment **F**.

DIY Repair Kit
- Seam ripper
- Pins
- Scissors
- Sewing machine
- Matching thread

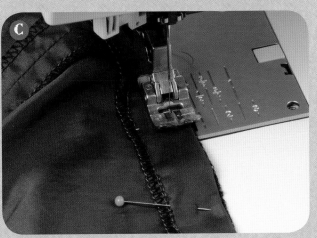

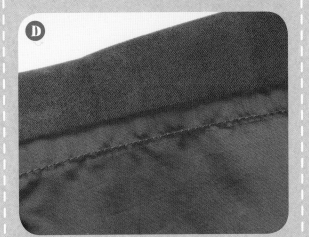

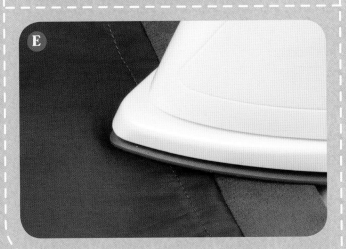

Letting down a hem

Letting down a hem on a skirt or a pair of trousers is only possible where the present hem has been turned up with a good hem allowance – in other words, there is some 'spare' fabric to 'let down'. Many cheaper, mass-produced garments are not made with this in mind and have the smallest of hems.

Step 1

Unpick the hem using a seam ripper or the point of sharp embroidery scissors **A**.

Step 2

Fill a water-spray bottle with 3fl oz (75ml) of distilled water. Add ¾fl oz (20ml) of white vinegar. Shake well then spray the hem fabric and the original fold with the solution **B**. NB: Do not spray pure silk or dry-clean-only fabrics. The vinegar helps to remove creases in woven fabrics. Cover the hem with a handkerchief or clean piece of fabric and press to make it smooth and flat.

If you are only letting down a small amount of the hem allowance, then you will conclude with step 3. If you require the full hem allowance to extend the length of your garment, however, then you will need to sew a strip of bias binding to the lower edge of the hem. To do this, after step 2 (above) follow the *alternate* step 3, followed by steps 4 and 5.

Step 3

Measure and then pin the hem to the desired length **C**. Press the fold of the hem with a warm iron. Sew the hem back into place using either slip stitch or herringbone stitch (see page 20 or pages 92–3).

Step 3 alternate

Open one folded edge of the bias binding and pin the bias to the free edge of the hem with right sides of fabrics touching **D**.

Step 4

Stitch the bias to the edge of the hem using straight stitch by hand or by machine-sewing in the crease of the bias fold **E**. The seam allowance will be approx. ¼in (5mm).

Step 5

The bias binding is now the hem of the garment. Turn up the bias to the inside of the garment. Press the hem flat with a warm iron, pin it into position **F** and then slip-stitch it to the garment to secure it in place.

DIY Repair Kit

- Water-spray bottle
  - 3fl oz (75ml) distilled water
  - ¾fl oz (20ml) white vinegar
- Handkerchief or pressing cloth
  - Iron
  - Needle
- Matching thread
  - Bias binding (if required)

Taking up a hem

Too often garments are discarded because they are too long. With fashion trends changing from season to season, hems go up and hems go down. With a little time and effort you can shorten the length of the hem of a skirt, dress or trousers following this simple procedure.

The best method of measuring to alter the hem of a garment is to put the garment on and ask a friend to mark the new hemline for you with chalk or by pinning all around. Short of a helping hand, have a look in a mirror while wearing the garment and make a pen or chalk mark on the garment where you want the new length to be. Take the garment off, measure up from the hemline to this mark and measure and mark a new hemline all around the item of clothing.

Step 1
Unpick the stitching along the original hem.

Step 2
Now measure down approximately 2in (5cm) from the mark where you wish the new hem to finish and mark the fabric where the excess hem needs to be cut off **A**. Mark all around the garment so that you have a clear line on which to cut and remove the excess material. Cut off the excess fabric.

Step 3
Fold under approx ½in (1cm) of the cut edge of the new hemline. Press the fold down with a warm iron. Turn the hem up to the new hemline marking and pin the hem evenly in place **B**.

Step 4
Using slip stitch or herringbone stitch (see pages 20 and 22), sew the fold of the hem fabric to the inside of the garment **C**. Press the fold of the hem when the stitching is completed.

DIY Repair Kit

- Iron
- Needle
- Matching thread
- Dressmaking chalk or water-soluble fabric-marker pen
- Tape measure or measuring gauge
- Scissors

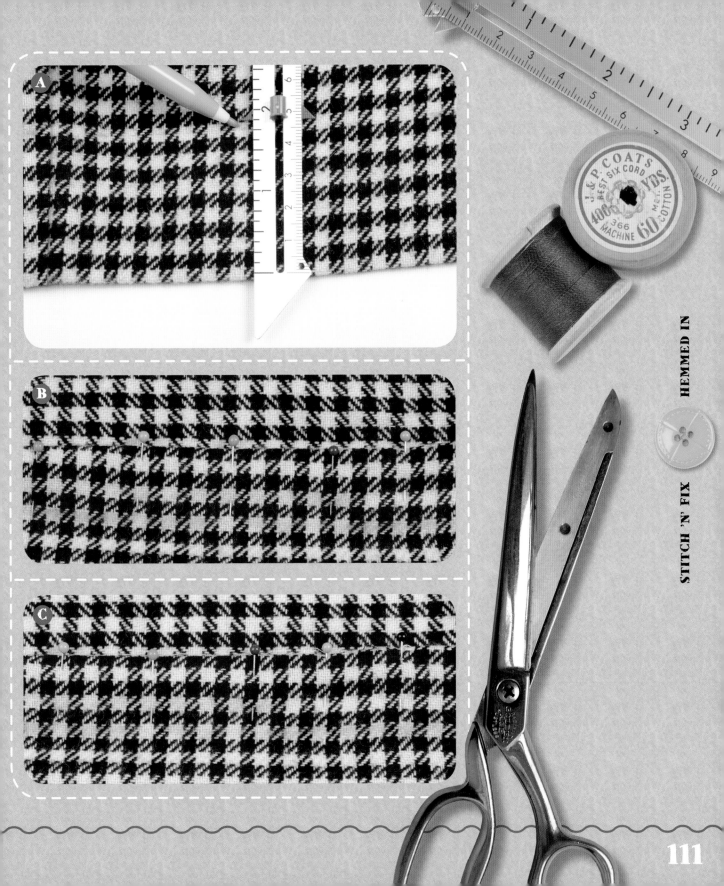

Concealing a permanent hemline mark

Occasionally when a hem has been let down, the fold mark of the original hem can't be removed by any amount of pressing or spraying with water and vinegar (see page 108). Some garments will lend themselves to having a trim sewn over the hemline mark, and this is the method shown here.

Decorative braids or ribbons are readily available in fabric and haberdashery shops. A length of braid, rickrack or woven ribbon can add a designer element to the hem of a skirt or dress. So this is where a repair can actually enhance the original garment and give it a whole new lease of life and individuality.

Attaching trim by hand

Step 1
Measure around the circumference of the hem and add 5in (13cm) for the length of braid.

Step 2
Pin the braid to the hem of the garment over the hem mark you wish to conceal **A**. Stitch it in place by hand with clear nylon thread using small slip stitches (see page 20) that are evenly spaced **B**.

Attaching trim by machine

Step 1
Measure around the circumference of the hem and add 5in (13cm) to this measurement for the length of braid.

Step 2
Set the machine to straight stitch. The length of the stitch is 1.5mm. Use transparent nylon thread on the upper thread spool of the machine and sewing thread that matches the fabric colour in the bobbin. Pin and then stitch the ribbon to the garment, ensuring that where the ribbon starts and finishes on the hem is neatly placed in line with the back seam of the garment **C**.

Step 3
Start sewing along the top of the ribbon. When you reach 2in (5cm) before the starting point of stitching, fold under the end of the ribbon to neaten it **D** and so that it aligns exactly with the back seam of the garment. Pin it so that the fold of the ribbon covers the raw edge of the underlying ribbon and stitch on and over the underlying ribbon. Back-stitch to secure. Now sew all around the lower edge of the ribbon **E**. Press the finished decorative ribbon with a warm iron.

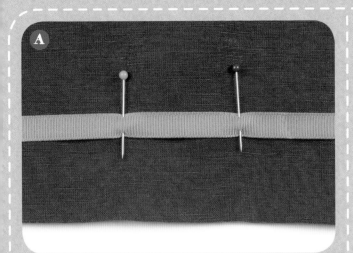

DIY Repair Kit

- Braid or ribbon
- Needle
- Transparent thread
- Scissors
- Pins
- Iron
- Sewing machine (optional)

Stitching a rolled hem on delicate fabric

A rolled hem is often used to neaten the hem of very fine fabrics such as silk, voile, georgette or lightweight polyester. This narrow hem allows the fabric to drape elegantly and is visually unobtrusive.

By hand

Step 1

To make a neat rolled hem, make a very narrow fold of no more than ¼in (6mm) along the edge of the fabric and pin in place. Press the fold with a warm iron **A**.

Step 2

Roll the fabric over again concealing the raw edge of the first hem. Pin the second fold in place **B**

Practical Pete says...

When working with slippery fabrics, spray starch onto the raw edge of the hem before rolling and pressing. It will give the fabric body, helping to hold it in place.

Step 3

Thread a needle with clear nylon thread and sew tiny slip stitches along the fold of the hem attaching it to the inside of the garment **C**. Secure the thread when sewing is completed with a neat knot, trim the excess using scissors and press the hem with a warm iron.

By machine

Step 1

Follow steps 1 and 2 for the sewing by hand method above. Set straight stitch to 2.5mm on your machine and sew along the very fold of the

hem on the inside of the garment **D**. Back-stitch to secure the stitching before trimming the threads. You will now have a neat machine-sewn hem **E**.

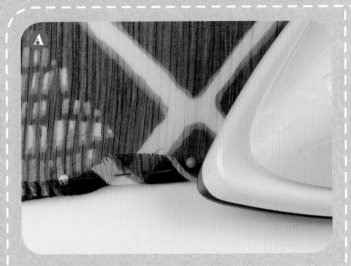

A

B

C

D

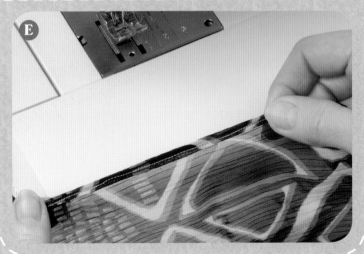

E

DIY Repair Kit

- Needle
- Thread
- Scissors
- Pins
- Sewing machine (optional)

Hemming stretch fabric with a sewing machine

Hemming stretch fabric by hand is inadvisable, as the stitching needs to be able to stretch with the fabric. If you must hem by hand, sew the garment with a narrow zigzag stitch on the inside using a polyester thread (see page 24).

Step 1
Pin the hem of the fabric to the inside of the garment **A**. Turn the garment over so that the right side is facing up. If you are unsure of where the end of the hem is now, draw a sewing line along the top surface of the fabric. This line will now be directly over the raw edge of the hem that has been pinned up.

Step 2
Attach the twin needle **B** to the machine. Thread the machine with both rolls of sewing thread and thread each eye of the needle separately with one strand of thread **C**. (*Two different coloured threads are shown in the photos, for clarity.*)

Step 3
Set your sewing machine to straight stitch with a length of 2.5mm. If you have drawn a sewing line on the top surface of the fabric (not shown in photo), line up the needles over the top of this line. The needles should be stitching over the raw edge of the hem on the inside of the garment **D**

Step 4
The needles sew a straight stitch on the right side of the material **E** but if you look at the inside of the garment you will see that the under-stitching is a zigzag stitch that stretches **F**

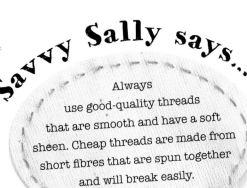

Savvy Sally says...

Always use good-quality threads that are smooth and have a soft sheen. Cheap threads are made from short fibres that are spun together and will break easily.

DIY Repair Kit
- Sewing machine
- Twin needle
- 2 rolls of sewing thread
- Scissors
- Pins

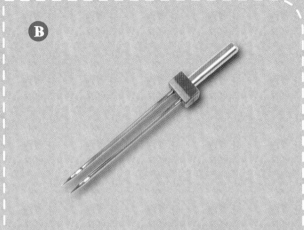

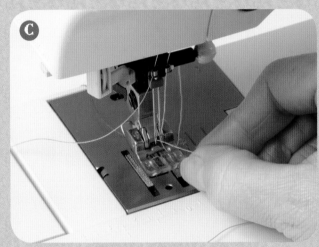

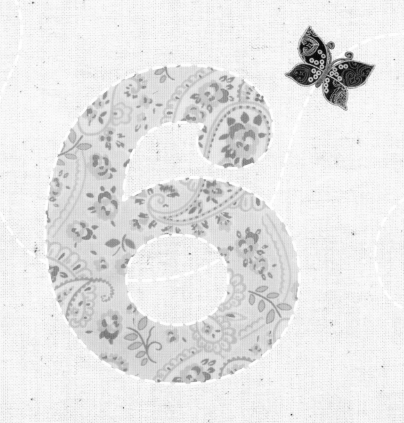

Luxury babe

Mending a broken bra strap

The elastic used to make bra straps will weaken with constant wear or may be stretched out of shape if it catches on the inside agitator of a washing machine. Elastic will also perish if it is exposed too often to chlorine or dried in tumble dryers. Replacement bra straps can be purchased from most haberdashery shops.

Replacement straps are usually sold in black, white and coffee colours **A**, which is rather limiting, but white straps can be dyed with fabric dyes if you need coloured straps to match a special bra. If the straps are to be dyed, ensure the bra is also placed in the dye solution at the same time as the straps to ensure a good colour match.

Step 1

Remove the original bra strap with scissors **B**. Most bras have a metal ring connector to which the strap is connected. Thread the new elastic strap through the metal ring, fold the elastic back on to itself and pin the end of the elastic to the inside edge of the strap **C**.

Step 2

Commence stitching with several little back stitches to secure the thread, sew the edge of the elastic to the strap using tiny back stitches and finish with several more stitches to ensure a secure join **D**. Now sew the free end of the strap to the front of the bra cup **E**. Adjust the strap to fit comfortably.

DIY Repair Kit
- Scissors
- Needle
- Matching thread
- Purchased bra straps
- Pins

Savvy Sally says...

Well-fitting bras are worth their weight in gold. A comfortable, lacy, sexy bra is a garment to be handled with care. Quality bras are expensive, so if you want a good return for your valued investment wash them by hand in a mild pure soap or shampoo solution and they will last for years.

Attaching a bra extension

Bra extenders are a brilliant invention – they eliminate tightness and any discomfort caused by pregnancy, weight gain or bra shrinkage. They consist of a piece of tape with one hook (or row of hooks) and several metal eyes stitched onto it. The extender hooks easily onto the back of the original bra fastening, thus giving you several more rows of hooks to 'let out' the bra.

Savvy Sally says...

Bra extenders come in single, double or triple width hooks and eyes **C**. They can be dyed to match the colour of your bra. Purchase fabric dye suitable for use on lingerie and follow the packet instructions.

Bra extenders

Bra extenders are available at most good quality bra shops or try haberdashery shops. If you can't find one, however, you can make one by sewing a hook and some eyes onto a length of fabric and attaching it to the back of your bra in the same way.

Step 1
Hook the extender to an eye (or row of eyes) on the back of the bra **A**.

Step 2
Hook the bra hooks to the eye on the extenders. An easy, no sew, do-it-yourself job done! **B**

Comfy straps

If you find that your bra straps dig into your shoulders causing discomfort, these comfy straps are ideal. They provide a cushioning effect that prevents rubbing and red marks. They can be purchased from most good haberdashery shops and are simple to slide over the bra strap **C**.

Bra extenders

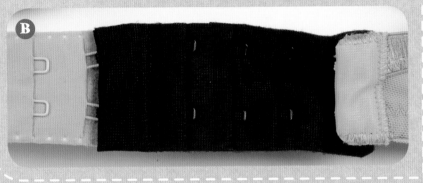

Comfy straps

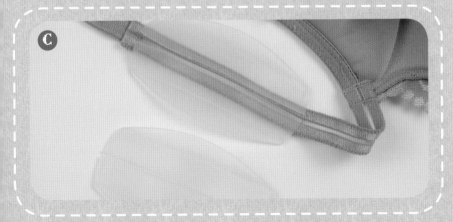

Preventing bra straps from sliding off shoulders

Narrow or sloping shoulders can be a frustration because they tend to mean your bra straps always slide off. Many of us pull the bra straps tighter and tighter, but this only causes the bra to ride up your back between your shoulder blades, inflicts discomfort and unsightly red marks and, ultimately, stretches the bra until it's unwearable. But nifty strap retainers sewn inside your favourite garments will solve all these problems!

Unfortunately, no one has yet invented some clever little gizmo to attach to a bra itself and prevent this common irritation. Rather, these retainers – simple loops of ribbon with snap fastenings **A** – need to be sewn inside the shoulders of your clothes, so that the straps can be threaded through them. They can be obtained at most good haberdashery or lingerie shops.

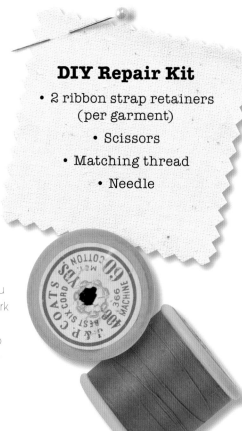

DIY Repair Kit
- 2 ribbon strap retainers (per garment)
- Scissors
- Matching thread
- Needle

Step 1
Try on the garment to which you wish to attach the retainers. Mark on the shoulder seam, with a pin, the position of the bra strap beneath the seam. Take off the garment, being careful not to dislodge the pin **B**.

Step 2
Open the retainer by unclipping the snap. Pin the middle of the ribbon to the inside shoulder seam of your garment where you marked it with a pin **C**.

Step 3
Thread a needle with sewing thread. Join both ends of thread with a simple knot. Sew the middle of the ribbon to the shoulder seam using back stitch. Try not to catch the top surface of the fabric. Attach the retainer to the seam allowance of the shoulder seam **D**.

Step 4
Try the garment on again. Slide the ends of the ribbon over and under the lingerie strap and press the snaps closed, holding the bra strap neatly in place **E**.

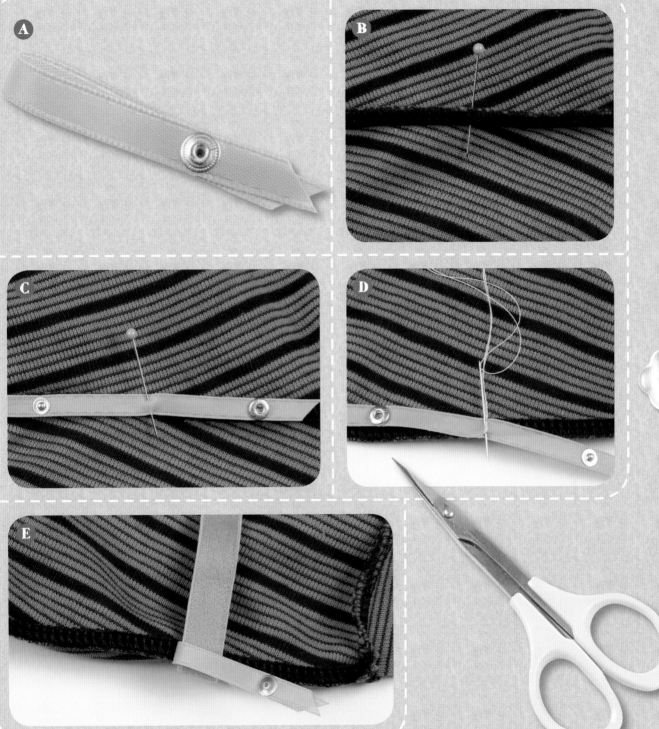

Repairing underwired bras

If you find wire-reinforced bra cups uncomfortable then it's quite simple to remove them altogether. Alternatively, if you do prefer the support provided by underwired bras, but the wires stick out of the casing and dig into your skin, then the simple repair described below will ensure a more comfortable fit.

Removing the wires from a bra

Step 1

To remove wire from the cup of a bra, snip a very small hole into the casing that holds it in place, as close to the upper side edge of the bra as possible **A**. Do not snip through the elastic. Slide the wire out **B**.

Step 2

Sew up the hole with a few neat little back stitches **C**.

DIY Repair Kit

- Needle
- Matching thread
- Scissors

Repairing protruding wires

Step 1

Wires often work their way through the soft casing that keeps them in place **D**. If the wires are protruding then push them back into the casing **E**.

Step 2

Thread a needle and tie a knot in the end of the two strands. Stitch over the hole in the casing, stitching back and forth over each stitch two or three times to close it securely **F**. Knot off the thread and trim any excess off with scissors.

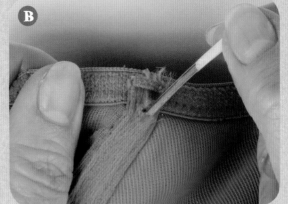

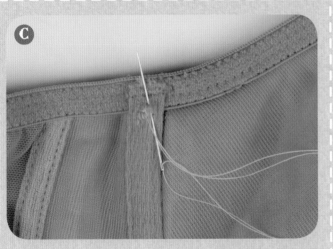

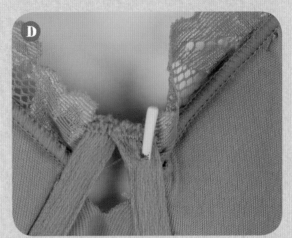

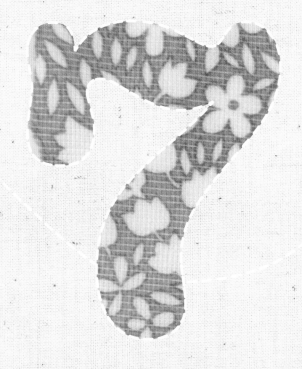

Fix it

Instant mending with iron-on interfacing

If you snag your shirt or the hem of your skirt and the fabric tears, don't despair. With a little piece of iron-on interfacing the damage can be fixed in a jiffy. Keep a small amount of white and black interfacing on hand for quick repairs.

Step 1
Gently press the torn fabric **A** so that the edges of the tear are touching **B**. Turn the garment inside out.

Step 2
Cut a piece of iron-on interfacing, slightly wider and longer than the tear in the fabric. Place the interfacing with the pre-glued side over the tear on the inside of the garment **C**.

Step 3
Cover the interfacing with a handkerchief or pressing cloth. Spray the covering cloth with a fine mist of water. Now press the iron firmly over the cloth, holding it in place for 30 seconds. Remove the cloth and check that the interfacing is fully adhered to the fabric. If it is not yet fully adhered, repeat the process but do not hold the iron down for more than 30 seconds at a time, in case it should scorch the fabric.

Step 4
Turn the garment right side out. If there are any frayed strands or fabric fibres showing, trim them off with scissors **D**.

DIY Repair Kit
- Iron-on interfacing
- Scissors
- Iron
- Water-spray bottle
- Handkerchief or pressing cloth

Practical Pete says...

Do not attempt this repair on dry-clean only fabrics.

131

Darning a hole

Darning figures pretty high on the drudgery list, right up there with the ironing, but it is such a useful skill to acquire – to repair all sorts of little holes or tears in your favourite garments. Put on some music, pour a glass of wine and settle into a comfortable chair to treat yourself while you do that darn darning!

Some little holes or tears can easily be repaired with iron-on interfacing, see pages 130–1. Others can be darned very quickly with a sewing machine. Some garments – those of a more intricate shape, the classic example being a sock with a hole in the toe – still need to be darned by hand.

Darning with a sewing machine

Step 1
Thread up your sewing machine with sewing thread to match the colour of the fabric (*contrasting thread is used in the photos, for clarity*) and set it to straight stitch with a stitch length of 1.5mm. Working widthways across the tear on the right side of the fabric, stitch back and forth across the tear, catching a few strands of fabric on each side. Continue until you have covered the tear, working in that one direction. When finished, cut off the end of the thread **A**.

Step 2
Turn the fabric approximately 90 degrees, and work back and forth over the original stitches to reinforce the repair. When finished stitching, secure the thread and snip off with scissors **B**.

Darning by hand

Step 1
Support the hole in the sock with your hand **A** or with a wooden darning dome. *Contrasting thread is used here for clarity.*

Step 2
With a threaded needle, make a series of small running stitches in one direction back and forth to close the hole **B**.

Step 3
In the same way, now stitch in the opposite direction to reinforce the repair **C**. Knot off and trim the thread close to the stitching.

Darning with a sewing machine

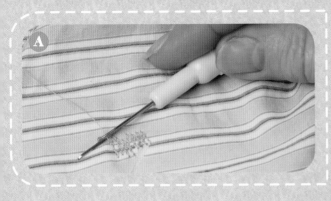

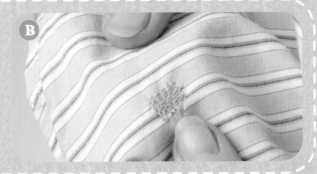

Darning by hand

Mending a pull in knitted fabric

A pulled yarn in a favourite knitted garment is not the end of the world. If the yarn is still intact and the stitch hasn't laddered through the rest of the garment, then it can be carefully pulled to the inside and neatly secured; that cosy vest or snug jumper can be repaired and enjoyed once again.

Step 1

Thread a needle and knot the two strands together. Isolate the area of the garment with the snag that you will be repairing **A**. The snag will most usually be on the outside of the garment. Stitch through the end of the pulled yarn. Make a small back stitch into the yarn to secure the thread into it **B**.

Step 2

Take the needle back into the hole from where the yarn was pulled **C** – through to the inside of the garment **D**.

Practical Pete says...

Knitted fabric can be easily pulled if the stitches are made wth a loose tension. Avoid wearing charm bracelets or jewellery with sharp edges that may catch the fibres of the knit.

Step 3

Ease the fabric of the garment gently with your fingers to remove any puckering on the outside. Now stitch the yarn to the inside of the garment closing the hole from whence it came, using neat little back stitches **E**. Trim off any excess thread with scissors. The repair should now be invisible from the outside of the garment **F**.

DIY Repair Kit

- Needle
- Matching thread
- Scissors

Stitching and covering a hole in stretch fabric

Stretch fabric isn't all that easy to repair. Once damaged it can ladder or become misshapen. The easiest way to mend a hole in stretch fabric is to cover it from the inside with a patch made from a similar fabric or to glue a decorative patch over the top of the hole.

Step 1
Cut a patch of fabric **A** sufficient in size to cover the hole in the damaged garment **B**

Step 2
Cut out a piece of iron-on hemming web the same size as the patch. Iron it on to the back of the patch, using a pressing cloth **C**.

Step 3
Place the patch on the inside of the garment with the hemming web against the hole **D**. Cover the patch with a pressing cloth and press it firmly with a warm iron for approximately 20–30 seconds.

Step 4
Turn the garment right-side out and check that the hole is completely repaired **E**.

DIY Repair Kit
- Hemming web
- Small patch of matching stretch fabric
- Scissors
- Iron
- Handkerchief or pressing cloth

Savvy Sally says...
You can also cover small holes with an iron-on decorative patch. See page 64 for how to make your own.

Invisible mending of loose-weave fabrics

If a valuable garment is damaged there are companies that specialize in invisible mending and it is worth doing some internet research into a company that may be able to assist you. For clothing, however, such as coats or jackets that may have been eaten by moths while in winter storage, an almost invisible DIY repair may still be achieved if the hole is very small.

Step 1
Isolate the small hole you need to repair **A**. Snip off a little of the fabric from an inside seam allowance where it's not visible **B**.

Step 2
Shred the fabric so that you have a little pile of fibres **C**. Chop up the fibres with scissors so that they become almost a powder **D**.

Step 3
Snip tiny shards of hemming web into the fibres and mix them together **E**. Carefully push the fibre mix into the hole on the garment, using the closed blades of a pair of dressmaking scissors **F**. Make sure the fibres are flush with the outside of the garment **G**.

Step 4
Now place a small piece of the hemming web over the hole. Cover the hole with a Teflon cooking sheet or baking parchment and press with a warm iron **H**. Move the iron over the covering for about ten seconds. Remove the covering, check that the fibres have melded into the hole.

Step 5
Turn the garment inside out and press a small patch of iron-on interfacing over the repaired hole to reinforce the repair **I**.

DIY Repair Kit
- Scissors
- Hemming web
- Small patch of iron on interfacing
- Baking parchment or Teflon sheet
- Iron

Removing and mending a damaged shirt pocket

Pockets on a business shirt often become damaged over time, as pens and wallets are slid in and out of them on a daily basis. Pens can also leak into the shirt and pocket fabric or the stitching can gradually become weakened and break through. In such cases, the pockets can either be permanently removed or easily repaired.

To completely remove a shirt pocket

Step 1

Using a seam ripper, carefully unpick the stitches from the wrong side of the garment **A**.

Step 2

Once all the stitching has been removed, spray the area with a mist of water and press. If there is still a stitch line or 'shadow' of where the pocket was, fill a water-spray bottle with 3fl oz (75ml) of distilled water.

Add ¾fl oz (20ml) of white vinegar. Shake well, then spray the fabric with the solution. **NB: Do not spray pure silk or dry-clean-only fabrics.** The vinegar helps to remove creases in woven fabrics. Cover the area with a piece of fabric and press.

To repair a shirt pocket

Step 1

To repair the stitching on a pocket, pin it back into position **B**. Thread a needle and tie a knot in one end of the thread. Pass the needle from the inside of the garment to the top surface, stitching over a few of the original stitches with back stitch to secure them.

Step 2

Continue to sew with neat, small and evenly tensioned back stitches until the pocket is firmly back into place **C**. Knot off the thread neatly on the inside of the shirt.

DIY Repair Kit

- Seam ripper
- Water-spray bottle
- 3fl oz (75ml) distilled water
- ¾fl oz (20ml) white vinegar
- Needle
- Matching thread
- Scissors
- Pins

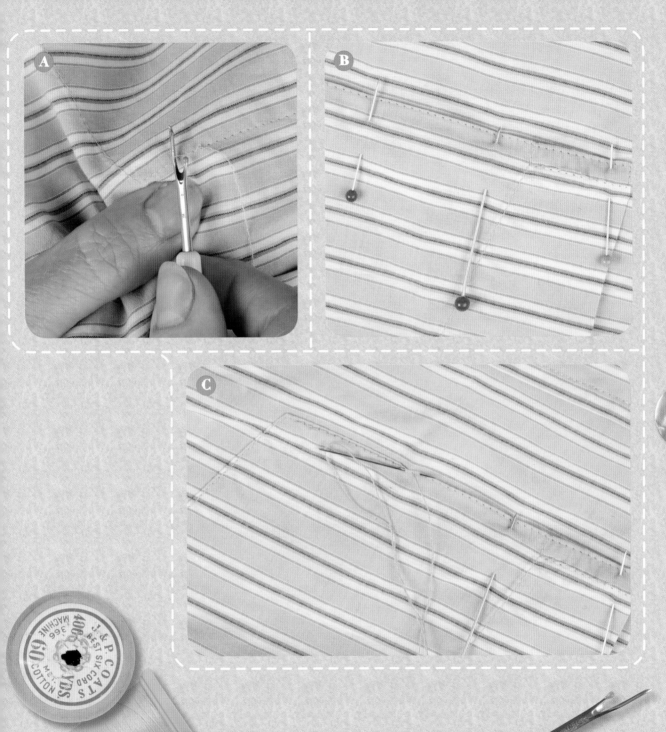

Reducing a gaping neckline

Do you find yourself always needing to add a pin or brooch to a gaping jumper neckline? Once the neckline of a knitted garment has been stretched it can't easily be put back into shape. If the body of the garment is still in good shape, however, you can reduce the amount of gaping by overstitching the edge of the neckline with buttonhole (blanket) stitch.

Practical Pete says...

To make a decorative finish, small seed beads can be threaded on as you stitch, which will add a sparkle to the repaired neckline.

You will probably want to practise doing buttonhole stitch (see page 20), before commencing a repair to a much-loved garment.

Step 1

Thread a needle with thread to match the colour of your garment (*contrasting thread is shown in the photos, for clarity*). Commence sewing at the shoulder seam. Sew small, neat, evenly spaced stitches along the edge of the neckline. Keep the tension of the thread fairly tight so that the excess ease in the neckline will be pulled back into shape **A**.

Step 2

When you have stitched all round the neckline and returned to your starting point, back-stitch on the inside to finish **B** and trim off the excess thread with scissors.

DIY Repair Kit
- Matching thread
- Needle
- Scissors

Creating an hourglass shape in a loose-fitting blouse

To give a more flattering silhouette to a blouse the side seams may be taken in at the waist to give the garment an hourglass shape. This is a simple procedure and can give an ill-fitting top a whole new look. The same technique can also be used on the side seams of dresses.

Step 1

Try the blouse on inside out and gradually pin in the side seams between the points approximately 5in (13cm) above the waist and 3in (7.5cm) below the waist. The seam should curve gradually in towards the waist and ease back out into the original seam. You can draw a nice gradual sewing line with fabric marker **A**. Before commencing sewing, check that you have taken in the same amount of fabric on each side of the blouse.

Step 2

Sew the seam by hand or machine using back stitch (see page 22). As you commence to sew, back-stitch in the same place to secure the thread and sew evenly spaced neat stitches along the new seam line **B**.

Step 3

Once the sewing is complete, make a few extra back stitches to secure the thread, then trim off the excess **C** Repeat Steps 2 and 3 on the other side seam. Press the seam to ensure the new stitching lies smooth and flat.

DIY Repair Kit

- Needle
- Matching thread
- Sewing machine (optional)
- Scissors
- Pins
- Fabric marker pen
- Tape measure

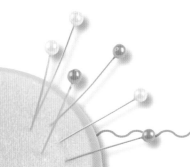

STITCH 'N' FIX   FIX IT

Stitching a bust dart into a top or blouse

Another way of creating a better shape in a loose-fitting blouse is to sew vertical darts from the hem to the bust point, on the inside of the front of the garment. This technique combines well with the technique for creating an hourglass shape in a blouse (see pages 144–5). Together these alterations can create a very shapely blouse.

Step 1

Try the blouse on inside out in front of a mirror. Pin a vertical dart from the hem of the blouse up towards the central point of the bust. The dart should be very narrow at the hemline, deepening towards the waist and petering out to nothing by the time you reach the bust point. Repeat on the other front panel of the blouse. Remove the blouse, try it on right-side out and re-pin before stitching if necessary, adding a sewing line in fabric marker pen if desired **Ⓐ**. Make sure that both darts are the same length, size and depth, and equidistant from the front central opening of the blouse, in order to keep the garment fitting symmetrically on each side. If the garment already has such darts in place, but they are not deep enough to fit you properly, you can take in these darts in exactly the same way.

Step 2

Back-stitch at the base of the dart to secure the thread. Sew the dart from the hem up to the end point, either by hand **Ⓑ**, using small neat back stitches, or with a sewing machine (also using back stitch, with a stitch length of 1.5mm). When the sewing is completed, carefully knot off the threads to secure the stitches. Repeat for the other dart.

Step 3

Press the darts with a warm iron. Clip a small V-shape into the dart at its widest part (which should be at the waist) **Ⓒ**, so the outer fabric can ease into the newly curved shape **Ⓓ**.

DIY Repair Kit

- Needle
- Matching thread
- Sewing machine (optional)
- Scissors
- Pins
- Fabric marker pen
- Tape measure

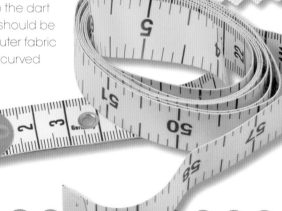

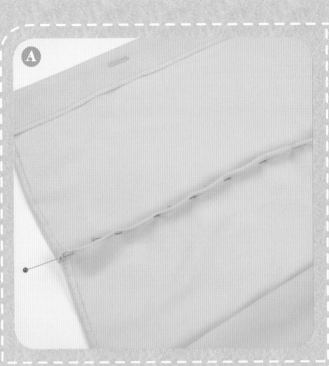

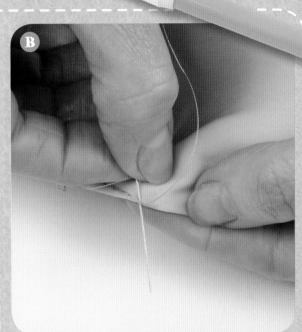

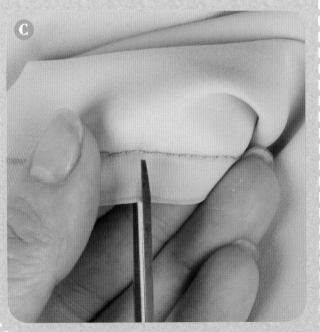

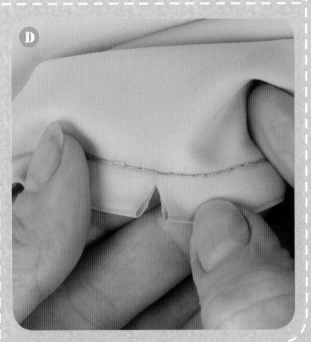

Preventing a saggy derrière in a skirt

The cut of a tight pencil skirt can be very flattering, but when the skirt is made from linen or loose-weave fabrics the derrière of the skirt can 'seat'. This means that the derrière section of the skirt stretches and shapes itself every time you sit down so that the fabric gradually becomes saggy and unflattering. Ironing interfacing into the skirt will prevent the derrière from stretching when worn and the back of your skirt will always look smooth and well fitting.

Step 1

Turn the skirt inside out and fit it over the ironing board so that the back of the skirt is facing towards you and the right side of the skirt is against the board. Measure from side seam to centre-back seam **A** and from the waist of the garment down towards the hem **B** approximately 13in (33cm).

Step 2

Transfer these measurements onto the interfacing **C** and **D**. Fold the interfacing in half so that as you cut out you have two matching pieces.

Step 3

Pin the interfacing onto the derrière of the skirt, starting just below the waistband **E**. With a warm iron gently press the interfacing onto the inside of the skirt. Slide the edges of the interfacing up to the side seams and press it flat and evenly into place. Cover the whole piece with a damp tea towel and press again firmly with the iron **F**. Continue until the interfacing is fused to the skirt. Repeat for both back sections of the skirt.

DIY Repair Kit

- Lightweight iron-on interfacing
- Iron
- Ironing board
- Scissors
- Tape measure
- Pins
- Fabric marker pen

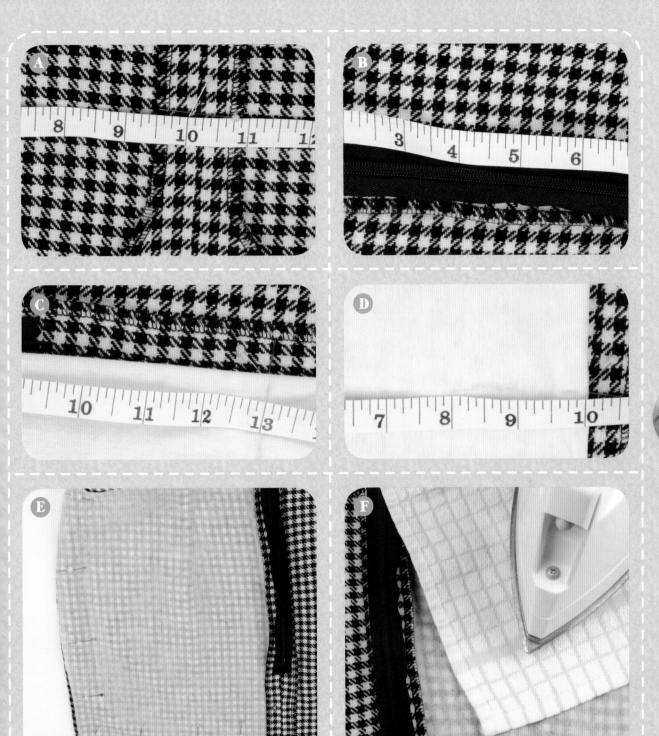

Alterations with shoulder pads

To remove shoulder pads from a jacket takes a little time and patience. If you have broad shoulders, removing the pads will make the shoulder seams fit more comfortably and look less bulky. Narrow shoulders will benefit from inserting shoulder pads, to add width to the upper body, creating a flattering line.

Removing shoulder pads

Step 1
Turn the jacket inside out. Carefully unpick the lining of the jacket at the shoulder seam using the seam ripper **A**. Start unpicking at the centre of the seam. Do not unpick the stitching all the way to the neckline or shoulder seam. Create an opening just big enough for you to access the shoulder pad.

Step 2
Unpick the stitching holding the shoulder pad into the inside of the garment **B**. Once the stitching has been removed slide the pad out. Slip-stitch (see page 20) the shoulder seam of the lining closed **C**.

Inserting shoulder pads

Step 1
An easy, no-sew, no-fuss method of inserting shoulder pads into a garment is to buy shoulder pads that have pre-glued, hook-and-loop (Velcro) detachable strip tapes. Place the flat side of the hook tape on the inside of the shoulder seam **D**. Cover it with a pressing cloth and iron it to the fabric pressing firmly for about 6–10 seconds **E**. The glue on the back of the tape will adhere itself to the garment.

Step 2
Try the garment on. Move the shoulder pad to the position you wish it to sit and press the shoulder seam of the garment firmly down onto the shoulder pad. The hook and loop tape will hold the pad in place **F**. Remove the pads when laundering the garment.

DIY Repair Kit
- Scissors
- Seam ripper
- Needle
- Matching thread
- Shoulder pads with hook-and-loop tape (optional)
- Iron
- Pressing cloth

Removing shoulder pads

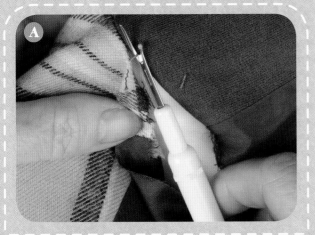

Inserting shoulder pads

Removing the waistband from a skirt

Some skirts are more comfortable without a waistband, especially for people with short-waisted figures. If you are such a person, you will no doubt have found that the waistband sits above your waist and not on your actual waistline, causing the skirt to crease up around the waistband.

Step 1
Using the seam ripper, unpick the waistband from the skirt **A**.

Step 2
Open one fold of bias tape and pin it to the original sewing line of the waistband on the outside of the skirt **B**.

Step 3
By hand or machine, use straight stitch to sew the bias tape to the skirt using neat, evenly spaced stitches **C**.

Step 4
Pin the tape to the inside of the garment encasing the raw edge. Press it smooth with a warm iron. Tuck in the cut edges at either end of the tape to neaten them **D**.

Step 5
Now slip-stitch (see page 20) the bias to the inside of the garment **E**, sealing each tucked-in end of the bias tape as you commence and finish sewing. Press the waistline of the skirt with a warm iron to finish.

DIY Repair Kit
- Seam ripper
- Scissors
- Bias binding
- Needle
- Matching thread
- Pins
- Sewing machine (optional)
- Iron

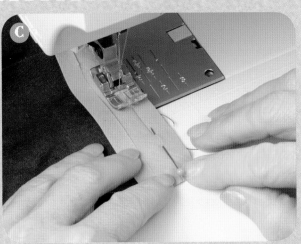

Expanding the waistband on a skirt or trousers

To expand the waistband on a skirt or trousers can be as easy as moving the button or metal closure so that you have a little more ease in the band to provide a more comfortable fit. Not everyone has a waist measurement that will fit ready-made clothing perfectly. Moving the button can make quite a difference.

STITCH 'N' FIX   FIX IT

Step 1
Try on the garment and if the zipper closes comfortably to the top of the skirt or trousers then you are in luck. The body of the garment fits you, but the waistband is too tight. Mark on the waistband with fabric marker pen the new position for the button or closure – perhaps right out at the end of the waistband **A**.

Step 2
Remove the button or metal closure with a seam ripper or sharp scissors **B**.

Step 3
Sew on the button or metal closure to the new position marked on the waistband **C**.

Step 4
Then secure the thread to the inside of the waistband **D**. You have now given yourself a little bit more breathing room at the waist **E**.

Savvy Sally says...
Change the button and use a decorative one that will add more interest to the closure.

DIY Repair Kit
- Scissors
- Needle
- Matching thread
- Fabric marker pen
- Seam ripper

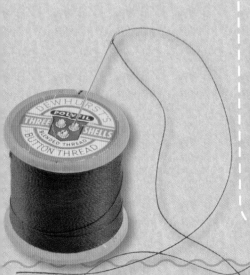

155

Reducing the waistband on a skirt or trousers

The easiest way of reducing the waistband on a skirt or trousers is to slash the waistband open and unpick the back seam of the garment. This of course is assuming that the back seam doesn't include a zipper. If the back seam does have a zip then you will need to remove the excess waistband in the side seams of the garment.

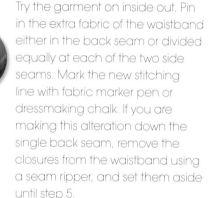

Step 1
Try the garment on inside out. Pin in the extra fabric of the waistband either in the back seam or divided equally at each of the two side seams. Mark the new stitching line with fabric marker pen or dressmaking chalk. If you are making this alteration down the single back seam, remove the closures from the waistband using a seam ripper, and set them aside until step 5.

Step 2
Carefully cut through the waistband to reach the stitching of the seam allowance. Unpick the stitching of the seam allowance from the waistline down into the seam(s) for at least 5in (13cm) **A**.

Step 3
Pin in the new seam following the marks on the inside of the garment that you made in step 1 **B**. Pin the excess fabric from the top of the seam to match the amount you wish to reduce from the waistband. Gradually pin down the seam, easing back out onto to the original seam.

Step 4
Now pin the waistband back onto the garment, using the marks as your guide **C**. Try the garment on before stitching the waistband and back or side seams securely together, using either back stitch or a sewing machine. Run a little fray-stop glue over the raw edges of the cut waistband to stop the fabric from fraying.

Step 5
If you have made this alteration down the single back seam of the garment, you will now need to reattach the waistband closures (button/metal fastener/hook and eye) to the ends of the new, shortened waistband.

DIY Repair Kit
- Seam ripper
- Scissors
- Needle
- Matching thread
- Dressmaking chalk or fabric marker pen
- Fray-stop glue

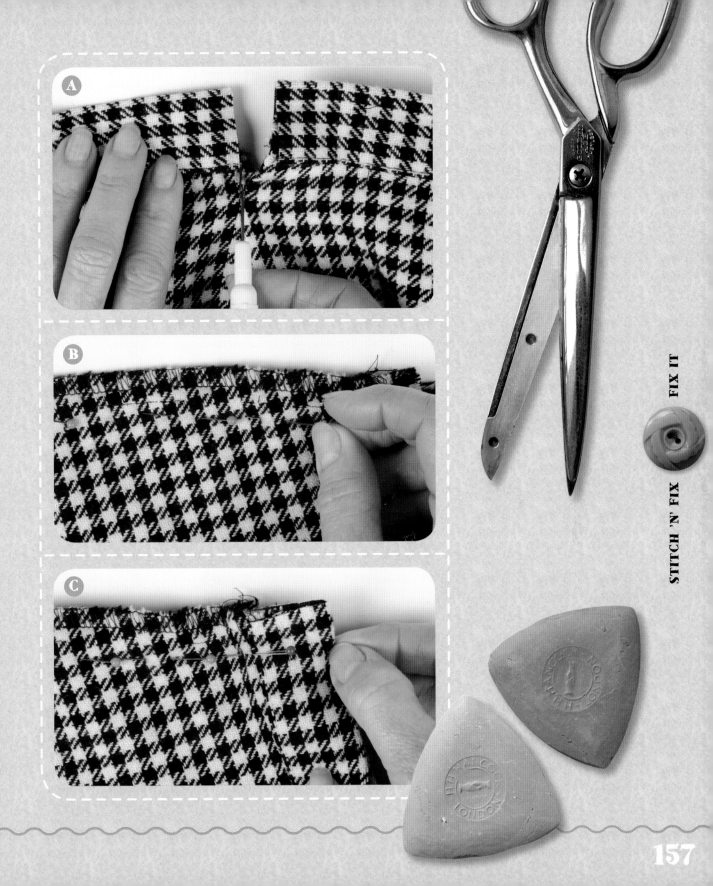

Replacing a drawstring

If the drawstring in the waistband of a garment – frequently tracksuit bottoms – has not been overstitched and it pulls out of the casing then it is quite a simple procedure to reinsert it into the waistband – and to prevent it working its way out again.

Step 1
Attach a safety pin to one end of the drawstring **A**.

Step 2
Insert the safety-pinned end of the drawstring into one of the holes, and using the safety pin to hold on to, ruche the waistband fabric over the string **B**, working it all the way round the waistband and out the other opening **C**.

Step 3
Create a large knot in each end of the drawstring **D** or thread on a bead and knot it in place to prevent the string from sliding inside the casing and working its way out again.

Practical Pete says...

Elastic may be threaded into the casing in a similar way and secured with a few quick stitches.

DIY Repair Kit
- Scissors
- Safety pin
- 2 beads (optional)

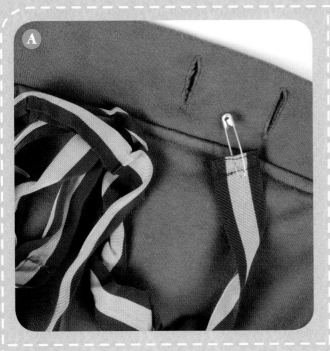

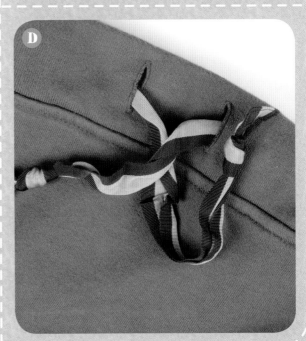

Fixing a zip pull

Zip pulls often dislodge from the top of the zip through wear and tear. You can replace a zip pull with another metal one or create your own fashion statement by attaching a bead or toggle to a jump ring.

Step 1
Open the jaws of the zip pull with chain-nose pliers, just sufficiently to clip it onto the zip **A**.

Step 2
Thread the ring back onto the zip pull. Holding one end of the ring in each pair of pliers, realign the ends to form a continuous ring **B**. Squeeze the jaws of the zip pull closed with either pair of pliers.

Step 3
Thread a needle with a double length of strong thread. Thread some decorative beads onto the needle **C** to create a row of the desired length. Pass the length of beads through the ring on the zip pull **D**.

Step 4
Thread the needle back through the row of beads and then knot off and secure with fray stop **E**.

Savvy Sally says...

Ready-made zip pulls can be purchased from bead shops and most haberdashery shops.

DIY Repair Kit
- Zip pull
- Chain-nose pliers
- Flat-nose pliers
- Needle
- Thread
- Beads
- Fray-stop glue

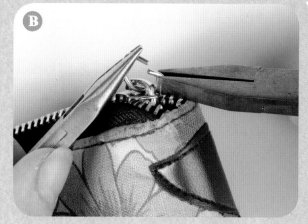

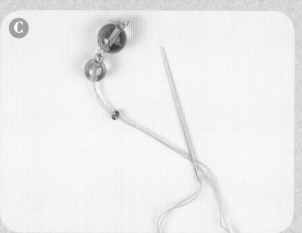

Removing a dart and creating a pleat to expand a garment

If the top section of a skirt or trouser is too tight just under the waistband – and the garment has darts – you can create more space for the tummy area by unpicking the darts and turning them into pleats. Or, if you have a very flat stomach, this technique will allow the fabric of the garment to hang neatly against your body.

Step 1
Unpick the stitches on the waistband either side of the dart with a seam ripper **A**

Step 2
Unpick the stitches on the dart **B** and press the fabric of the dart flat with a warm iron.

Step 3
Fold the excess fabric at the top of the unpicked dart into a pleat and pin in place **C**

Step 4
Slide the pleat back into the opening of the waistband and pin back in place **D**. Neatly stitch the waistband closed again, either by hand, using tiny straight stitches of equal length **E**, or by machine.

Practical Pete says...

To stop pleats from gaping, top-stitch them down with small running stitches.

DIY Repair Kit
- Seam ripper
- Needle
- Matching thread
- Iron
- Sewing machine (optional)

Turning a pleat into a dart

If the pleat on a garment gapes and looks unattractive then it can be stitched into a dart, which will make the fabric sit smoothly against the body. A dart will also create a curve in the fabric that may better accomodate a full tummy or bust.

Step 1
Unpick a small section of the waistband either side of the pleat to gain access to the stitching that holds the pleat in place **A**.

Step 2
Pin the fabric of the pleat into a dart **B**. The bulk of the pleat at the top should be folded into equal halves. Taper off the end of the pleat into a neat point.

Step 3
Stitch the pleat into a neat dart **C** either by hand, using tiny running stitches, or a sewing machine. Secure the thread at the commencement and end of stitching with a neat back stitch.

Step 4
Press the dart towards the side seam so that it lies flat. Slide the dart carefully back into the opening of the waistband, pin in place, then stitch the waistband closed **D**.

Savvy Sally says...

Darts are sewn into garments to make the fabric fit a certain part of the body. If you have a rounded tummy, a dart in a skirt will allow the fabric to drape more comfortably over your figure.

DIY Repair Kit
- Seam ripper
- Needle
- Matching thread
- Iron
- Sewing machine (optional)
- Pins

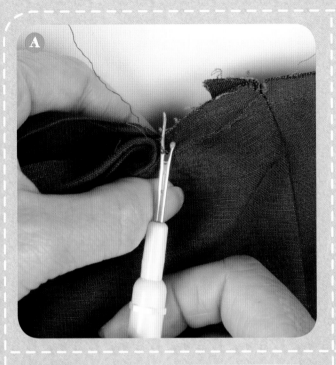

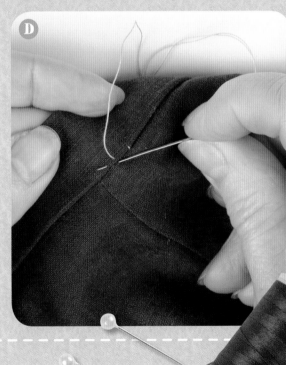

Suppliers

UK

Crowson and Monkwell Fabrics
Crowson House
Bellbrook Park
Uckfield
East Sussex
TN22 1QZ
Tel: 01825 761055
www.crowsonfabrics.com

Fabrics for Perfect Occasions
Woodhead Road
Bradford
West Yorkshire
BD7 1PB
Tel: 01274 414887
www.perfectoccasions.co.uk

Groves & Banks
Drakes Drive Industrial Estate
Long Credon
Aylesbury
Bucks
HP18 9BA
Tel: 01844 258080
www.groves-banks.com

Perival Gutermann
Bullsbrook Road
Hayes
Middlesex
UB4 0JR
www.gutermann.com

Janome Sewing Machines
Janome Centre
Southside
Stockport
Cheshire
SK6 2SP
Tel: 0161 666 6011
www.janome.co.uk

John Kaldor Fabricmaker (UK) Ltd
Centro 4
20–23 Mandela Street
Camden
London
NW1 0DU
Tel: 020 7874 5070
www.johnkaldor.co.uk

John Lewis
Oxford Street
London
W14 1EX
Tel: 020 7629 7711
www.johnlewis.com

Rufflette Ltd (UK)
Sharston Road
Manchester
M22 4TH
Tel: 0161 998 1811
www.rufflette.com

Simplicity Ltd (UK)
PO Box 367
Coronation Street
Stockport
Cheshire
SK5 7W2
Tel: 0161 480 8734
www.simplicity.com

Some more online suppliers are:
www.truetrim.com
www.jaycotts.co.uk
www.jaytrim.com
www.candh.co.uk
www.sewingcrafts.co.uk
www.sewingmachine-sales.co.uk
www.calicolaine.co.uk
www.habbyworld.co.uk
www.ladysewandsew.com
www.sewingmachines.co.uk
www.sewing.co.uk
www.ribbonmoon.co.uk
www.millcroftextiles.com
www.hobbycraft.co.uk

SUPPLIERS

STITCH 'N' FIX

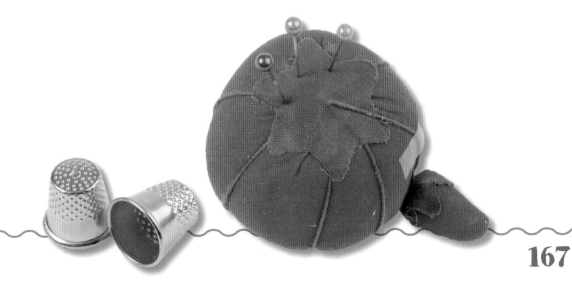

US

Brewer Quilting & Sewing Supplies
3702 Prairie Lake Court
Aurora
IL 60504
Tel: 630 820 5695
www.brewersewing.com

Guterman of America Inc
PO Box 7387
Charlotte
NC 28241-7387
Tel: 704 525 7068
www.gutermann.com

Janome Sewing Machines
10 Industrial Avenue
Mahwah
NJ 07430
Tel: 800 631 0183
www.janome.com

Simplicity Pattern Co Inc (USA)
2 Park Avenue, 12th Floor
New York
NY 10016
Tel: 212 372 0500
www.simplicity.com

Textol Systems Inc (Rufflette USA)
435 Meadow Lane
Carlstadt
NJ 07072
Tel: 800 624 8746
www.textol.com

Australia

Lincraft
56 Rosebank Avenue (Head Office)
Clayton South
Victoria 3169
Tel: 1300 730 140
www.lincraft.com.au

Simplicity Pty Limited
25 Violet Street
Revesby
NSW
Tel: 2 9774 5855
www.simp.com.au

Spotlight
Head Office
111 Cecil Street
South Melbourne
Victoria 3205
Tel: 1300 305 405
www.spotlight.com.au

South Africa

Lifestyle Fabrics, Curtain and Linen
11 Picton Road
Parow
Cape Town
Tel: 021 930 5170

Durban
Classic Textiles
126 Archary Road
1st Floor
Clairwood
Durban 4052
Tel: 031 465 9016
www.classictextiles.co.za

New Zealand

Spotlight Stores
Christchurch (03) 377 6121
Dunedin (03) 477 1478
Invercargill (03) 211 1822
Hamilton (07) 839 1793
Hastings (06) 878 5223
Henderson (09) 836 0888
Manukau City (09) 263 6760
New Plymouth (06) 757 3575
Palmerston North (06) 357 6833
Panmure (09) 527 0915
Porirua (04) 238 4055
Rotorua (07) 343 6901
Wairau Park (09) 444 0220
Wellington (04) 472 5600
Whangarei (09) 430 7220
www.spotlight.co.nz

SUPPLIERS

STITCH 'N' FIX

Glossary

Bias binding Narrow strip of fabric cut on the bias (i.e. at 45 degrees to the straight grain) and therefore stretchable, pressed with folds for easy application, used to finish raw fabric edges.

Dart A stitched fold in fabric that is wider at the starting point and ends in a sharp point. It is used in dressmaking to create shape in a garment.

Dressmaking chalk Chalk that is used to make markings on fabric. The chalk may be dusted off the fabric once the marks are no longer needed. Available in pencil or stick form.

Fusible bonding A web of non-woven fibres that are usually backed with paper, which may be melted with an iron to attach fabric to fabric. Often used in appliqué techniques.

Hemming web Narrow strips of non-woven fibres that may be melted with an iron to join two fabrics together.

Interfacing May be a non-woven or woven fabric that is fused or stitched to the back of fabric to stabilize it and prevent the fabric from distorting in use or during stitching.

Linen A natural-fibre woven fabric available in a variety of different weights and textures.

Pressing cloth A piece of cotton fabric used to prevent the iron from scoring fabric.

Pure silk Natural-fibre woven fabric with a lustrous finish available in various weights. The weight for silk is termed 'mummy'.

Seam ripper Also called a 'quick unpick'. A small tool with a curved blade. The point of the blade slides under the stitch and the curve cuts through the thread. It is used for unpicking stitching.

Tape measure A pliable tape that is marked with measurements. It is used to ascertain the length, width, height or circumference of a given object or person.

Transparent nylon thread This thread is readily used in manufacturing. The thread is ideal for sewing emergency repairs as it doesn't have to be colour matched to the fabric.

Wash-away pen A felt-tipped pen filled with either a blue or pink ink that dissolves when it makes contact with water. Used for temporary markings on fabric.

Conversion chart

Inches	Centimetres
½	1.3
1	2.5
2	5.1
3	7.6
4	10.2
5	12.7
6	15.2
7	17.8
8	20.3
9	22.9
10	25.4
11	27.9
12	30.5

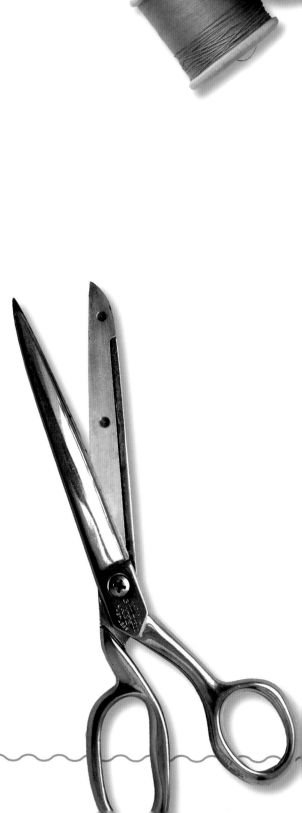

About the author

Joan Gordon is an international consultant who has taught various crafts and sewing techniques throughout Australia, New Zealand and the UK. Joan is passionate about exploring traditional and contemporary jewellery, craft and sewing skills and shares her knowledge with all generations.

For several years she was the Queensland State Manager for McCalls Patterns in Australia and later created her own business 'Victorian Lady'. Before leaving to work in the UK, Joan was the national promotions and sewing co-ordinator for Kwik.Sew patterns in Brisbane.

As a sewing and design consultant Joan is currently working and writing for publishing and exhibition companies in the UK. Several times a year she enjoys teaching jewellery and sewing workshops in her studio at The Model House, Llantrisant, Wales.

Joan has co-ordinated and featured in four bead- and jewellery-focused DVDs, written for many magazines including *Australian Stitches, Popular Crafts, Sewing World, Craft Beautiful, Simply Cards and Paper, Making Cards* and *My Weekly* and is the author of *The Silk Ribbon Embroidery Bible* (Quarto publications). She has also co-designed and edited the UK craft magazine *Beads & Beyond* for Traplet Publications and is now the Consultant Editor for the innovative UK jewellery magazine *Making Jewellery* for GMC Publications.

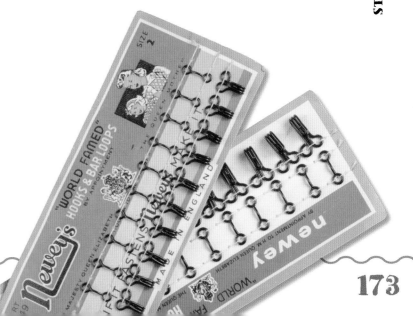

Index

FIX IT

STITCH 'N' FIX

To place an order, or to request a catalogue, contact:

GMC Publications Ltd

Castle Place, 166 High Street, Lewes, East Sussex, BN7 1XU
United Kingdom
Tel: 01273 488005   **Fax:** 01273 402866
Website: www.gmcbooks.com
Orders by credit card are accepted